# Regents English Workbook 1
## Beginning – New Edition

*Robert J. Dixson*

*Prentice Hall Regents*
Englewood Cliffs, New Jersey 07632

**Library of Congress Cataloging-in-Publication Data**

Dixson, Robert James.
    Regents English workbook 1 : beginning / Robert J. Dixson,
  -- New ed.
      p.   cm.
    ISBN 0-13-199001-2 :
    1. English language--Textbooks for foreign speakers.  2. English
language--Grammar--Problems, exercises, etc.  I..
II. Title.   III. Title: Regents English workbook one.
PE1128.D523  1995
428.2'4--dc20
                                                            94-47009
                                                               CIP

Acquisitions Editor: *Nancy Baxer*
Director of Production and Manufacturing: *David Riccardi*
Editorial Production/Design Manager: *Dominick Mosco*
Editorial/Production Supervision and Interior Design: *Dit Mosco*
Cover Art & Design Coordinator: *Merle Krumper*
Cover Design: *Laura C. Ierardi*
Production Coordinator: *Ray Keating*

©1995 by R.J. Dixson Associates
Published by Prentice Hall Regents
Prentice-Hall, Inc.
A Simon & Schuster Company
Englewood Cliffs, New Jersey 07632

Printed in the United States of America
10  9  8  7  6  5  4  3

ISBN 0-13-199001-2

Prentice-Hall International (UK) Limited, *London*
Prentice-Hall of Australia Pty. Limited, *Sydney*
Prentice-Hall Canada Inc., *Toronto*
Prentice-Hall Hispanoamericana, S.A., *Mexico*
Prentice-Hall of India Private Limited, *New Delhi*
Prentice-Hall of Japan, Inc., *Tokyo*
Simon & Schuster Asia Pte. Ltd., *Singapore*
Editora Prentice-Hall do Brasil, Ltda., *Rio de Janeiro*

There is no need here to describe the different types of exercises which this book contains or to discuss their wide variety and extent. A glance through the following pages is enough to acquaint anyone with the book's general contents.

Since this is a workbook, there is also little to say as to how it should be used. Each exercise carries its own instructions, and the students proceed accordingly. On the other hand, there are a few points of general pedagogy which the teacher using the book should keep in mind.

First, this is a workbook, and all explanatory material has been kept to a minimum. Thus, the book is not designed to be used alone or to replace completely the regular classroom text. Rather, this book should be used to supplement the regular classroom text, to give needed variety to the lesson, or to provide additional drill materials on important points of grammar and usage.

Second, as a teacher using this book, don't assume that after students have written the answers to an exercise correctly, they know the material thoroughly and can use the principle in their everyday speech. The exercise is often only the beginning. Much drill and practice are still necessary. Therefore, ask questions or introduce simple conversation involving the particular grammar principle. Also, don't hesitate to repeat the exercises in the book several times. Run over these exercises orally in class. If the students have already written the answers in their books, they can cover these answers with their hand or with a separate sheet of paper. Continue to review past exercises which seem important to you or which have given the students difficulty.

Third, don't fall into the further error of assuming that some of the exercises in this book are too easy for your particular students. Certain exercises may seem easy to you—especially if you speak English as a native—but they still represent a real challenge to anyone studying English as a foreign language. In this connection, there is one additional point of utmost importance which should be kept in mind. We are not interested in these exercises in tricking or even in **testing** the student. The exercises are not designed to find out how much a student knows or does not know. Their purpose is simply to drill the student on certain basic points of grammar and usage. The exercises are practice exercises—nothing more. They provide just another means of having students repeat materials which can be learned only through continuous use. For this reason, the exercises have been made as simple ans as clear as possible. For the same reason a good deal of direct repetition has been purposely introduced, not only in individual exercises but throughout the book.

There are three workbooks in the series. Book 1 is for the beginning student; Book 2 is for the intermediate student; Book 3 is for the advanced student. As regards the exact division of material, this plan was followed: The exercises in Book 1 more or less parallel the development by lesson of the material in **Beginning Lessons in English** A and B. Similarly, Book 2 follows the general development of the lessons in **Second Book in English**. Book 3 reviews the material in Books 1 and 2 and focuses on special problems on the advanced level. All the books mentioned are published by Prentice Hall Regents.

**Regents English Workbooks** are readily adaptable to many uses and can serve effectively to supplement any standard classroom textbook. A perforated answer key at the back of the book makes classroom use or self-study equally feasible.

R.J.D.

# Contents

# 1  *To be:* present tense 1

**The verb** to be **has these forms in the present tense. Contractions are generally used in spoken English.**

| Full Form | Contraction | Full Form | Contraction |
|-----------|-------------|-----------|-------------|
| I am | I'm | we are | we're |
| you are | you're | you are | you're |
| he is | he's | they are | they're |
| she is | she's | | |
| it is | it's | | |

*Write the correct form of the present tense of* to be *in the blanks. Use the contracted form with the personal pronouns.*

1. I _____ a student.          *I'm*
2. Dennis _____ a student.    _____
3. This _____ a good book.    _____
4. John and Pat _____ good students.    _____
5. They _____ in my class.    _____
6. He _____ a good teacher.    _____
7. You _____ a good student.    _____
8. I _____ tired now.    _____
9. We _____ in class now.    _____
10. Maria _____ at work today.    _____
11. She _____ a good student.    _____
12. Today _____ Monday.    _____
13. It _____ a beautiful day.    _____
14. You and Henry _____ brothers.    _____
15. They _____ in my class.    _____

## 2    *To be:* present tense 2

*Select the correct form. Write your answer in the blanks.*

1.  John (is, are) a good student.            *is*
2.  We (am, are) good students.        _____
3.  Today (is, are) Monday.        _____
4.  This (is, are) a good exercise.        _____
5.  William and George (is, are) brothers.        _____
6.  They (is, are) good students.        _____
7.  I (am, is) a student of English.        _____
8.  The window (is, are) open.        _____
9.  Both doors (is, are) closed.        _____
10.  Ana and I (am, are) in the same class.        _____
11.  We (am, are) brothers.        _____
12.  Miss Smith (is, are) a teacher.        _____
13.  She (is, are) a very good teacher.        _____
14.  Mr. Jones (is, am) a teacher.        _____
15.  He (is, are) also a good teacher.        _____
16.  Mr. and Mrs. Rizzoli (is, are) North Americans.        _____
17.  You (am, are) a good student.        _____
18.  I (am, is) also a good student.        _____
19.  The weather today (is, are) good.        _____
20.  This (is, are) a good exercise.        _____
21.  She and Mary (is, are) sisters.        _____
22.  You and Henry (is, are) brothers.        _____

**Form the negative of** to be **by putting** not **after the verb. Note the contractions.**

| | |
|---|---|
| I *am not* a teacher. | *I'm not* a teacher. |
| You *are not* a teacher. | You *aren't* a teacher. |
| He *is not* here. | He *isn't* here. |
| She *is not* a good student. | She *isn't* a good student. |
| We *are not* late. | We *aren't* late. |

*Change to the negative form. Use contractions wherever possible.*

1.  We are brothers. — *aren't*
2.  Today is Monday. — _____
3.  She and Mary are sisters. — _____
4.  I am a good speaker. — _____
5.  This is a difficult exercise. — _____
6.  Miss Jones is a good skater. — _____
7.  Mr. and Mrs. Bielski are North Americans. — _____
8.  She is a good friend. — _____
9.  They are busy today. — _____
10.  You and Henry are cousins. — _____
11.  John and I are in the same class. — _____
12.  Juan is busy today. — _____
13.  We are busy today. — _____
14.  Henry and he are first cousins. — _____
15.  You are a good student. — _____
16.  You and George are good friends. — _____
17.  Mary and I are good friends. — _____
18.  The door is closed. — _____
19.  Both windows are open. — _____
20.  They are brothers. — _____
21.  We are friends. — _____

# 4   *To be:* question form

***Form questions with*** to be ***by placing the verb before the subject.***

> *Is* she a good student?
>
> *Are* you and Henry cousins?

*Change to the question form. Write the verb and subject in the blanks.*

1. They are tennis players.          *Are they*
2. He is a bad student.         _____
3. Today is Tuesday.         _____
4. Antonia and he are in the same class.         _____
5. You and George are good students.         _____
6. She and Mary are good friends.         _____
7. The windows are closed.         _____
8. The door is wide open.         _____
9. They are new students.         _____
10. Henry and she are dancers.         _____
11. We are busy today.         _____
12. Mr. and Mrs. Jones are British.         _____
13. This is a difficult exercise.         _____
14. This lesson is easy.         _____
15. She is a good teacher.         _____
16. Joe and he are brothers.         _____
17. You and Henry are in the same class.         _____
18. They are tired today.         _____
19. The teacher is tired.         _____
20. This is a good book.         _____
21. They are old friends.         _____
22. He is a tall man.         _____

# 5 To have: present tense

| | |
|---|---|
| I have | we have |
| you have | you have |
| he has | they have |
| she has | |
| it has | |

*Write the correct form of to have in the blanks.*

1. Helen _____ a new hat.                                    *has*
2. I _____ many friends in this class.                       _____
3. We _____ new English books.                               _____
4. You _____ a good tape recorder.                           _____
5. The dog _____ a long tail.                                _____
6. This book _____ a red cover.                              _____
7. I _____ a new sports car.                                 _____
8. Mary _____ a new stereo.                                  _____
9. John _____ a new watch.                                   _____
10. John and Henry _____ many friends.                       _____
11. We _____ pencils but no pens.                            _____
12. I _____ two sisters but no brothers.                     _____
13. John _____ two brothers but no sisters.                  _____
14. Miss Stein _____ a new typewriter.                       _____
15. The teacher _____ red hair.                              _____
16. You _____ brown eyes.                                    _____
17. I _____ blue eyes.                                       _____
18. The cat _____ green eyes.                                _____
19. We all _____ new clothes.                                _____
20. George and I _____ new ties.                             _____
21. This room _____ many windows.                            _____

# 6　To have: negative form

**To form the negative of** to have, **place** do not **or** does not **before the verb. The contracted forms** don't **and** doesn't **are normally used.**

| | |
|---|---|
| They have a nice car. | They *do not (don't)* have a nice car. |
| I have a new house. | I *do not (don't)* have a new house. |
| He has two radios. | He *does not (doesn't)* have two radios. |

*Change to the negative form. Use the contracted forms.*

1.　She has a new hat.　　　　　　　　　　　　　　*doesn't have*
2.　They have many friends in the United States.　　_____
3.　Helen has red hair.　　　　　　　　　　　　　_____
4.　The cat has three kittens.　　　　　　　　　　_____
5.　That room has a broken window.　　　　　　　_____
6.　Rita has a bad cold.　　　　　　　　　　　　　_____
7.　I have two sisters.　　　　　　　　　　　　　　_____
8.　John has two brothers.　　　　　　　　　　　　_____
9.　This book has good photos.　　　　　　　　　　_____
10.　We have two different English books.　　　　　_____
11.　He has a new car.　　　　　　　　　　　　　　_____
12.　The men have their coats on.　　　　　　　　　_____
13.　John has his coat off.　　　　　　　　　　　　_____
14.　Helen has blue eyes.　　　　　　　　　　　　　_____
15.　I have a dog.　　　　　　　　　　　　　　　　_____
16.　Mary has a cat.　　　　　　　　　　　　　　　_____
17.　The cat has a short tail.　　　　　　　　　　　_____
18.　The dog has a long nose.　　　　　　　　　　　_____
19.　I have a good TV set.　　　　　　　　　　　　_____
20.　John and Henry have many friends in this class.　_____

# 7   *To have:* question form

**To form questions with** to have, **place** do **or** does **before the subject.**

| | |
|---|---|
| I have a good camera. | *Do* you have a good camera? |
| Lydia has new sunglasses. | *Does* Lydia have new sunglasses? |
| We have enough time. | *Do* we have enough time? |

*Change to the question form. Write the verb and subject in the blanks.*

1.   She has a new apartment.                          *Does she have*
2.   This room has three doors.                         _____
3.   That girl has very long hair.                        _____
4.   You have a dog.                                       _____
5.   Helen has many friends in this class.            _____
6.   The cat has a long tail.                              _____
7.   These dogs have long noses.                       _____
8.   Mary has brown eyes.                                _____
9.   You have a bad cold today.                         _____
10.  Mr. Shapiro has his coat off.                       _____
11.  John has his hat on.                                 _____
12.  We have different English books.                  _____
13.  This book has a blue cover.                          _____
14.  Mr. Smith has a new briefcase.                     _____
15.  You have a new watch.                               _____
16.  Most watches have two hands and a face.        _____
17.  Every student in the class has a radio.            _____
18.  We have new tennis equipment.                    _____
19.  Helen has a bad headache.                          _____
20.  Miss Pappas has a new sports car.                 _____

*The simple present tense describes an action which goes on every day or in general. In the third person singular, s is added to the verb.*

| | |
|---|---|
| I work | we work |
| you work | you work |
| he works | they work |
| she works | |
| it works | |

*Write the correct form of the verb in parentheses in the blanks.*

1. John (speak) English well.      *speaks*
2. We (write) many letters. _____
3. I (walk) to school with John every day. _____
4. Henry (walk) to school with Mary. _____
5. I always (sit) in this seat. _____
6. Henry always (sit) in that seat. _____
7. The students (write) many exercises every day. _____
8. John always (open) the windows for the teacher. _____
9. Ms. Barbero (work) in this room. _____
10. He (smoke) many cigarettes. _____
11. I (come) to school by bus. _____
12. Henry also (come) to school by bus. _____
13. George and his brother (walk) to school. _____
14. I (read) the newspaper every day. _____
15. We (eat) in the cafeteria every day. _____
16. Mr. Smith also (eat) in the cafeteria every day. _____
17. I (play) tennis every afternoon. _____
18. Diego also (play) tennis every afternoon. _____
19. Many students (play) tennis every afternoon. _____
20. Helen (work) very hard. _____
21. She (want) to learn English. _____

# 9    Simple present tense 2

**Add** s *to form the third person singular of most verbs. Add* es *instead of* s *in the following cases:*

| | |
|---|---|
| a. | when the verb ends in *o*<br>go-goes   do-does |
| b. | when the verb ends in *s*, *sh*, *ch*, *x*, or *z*<br>teach-teaches   wash-washes   fix-fixes |
| c. | when the verb ends in *y* (In this case, the *y* is changed to *i* before adding *es* if the *y* is preceded by a consonant.)<br>study-studies   cry-cries   marry-marries |

*Select the correct form. Write your answer in the blanks.*

1.  I (study, studies) English every day.                                  *study*
2.  John also (study, studies) English every day.                    _____
3.  Tran (go, goes) to the movies very often.                          _____
4.  I seldom (go, goes) to the movies.                                     _____
5.  William (carry, carries) his books in a briefcase.            _____
6.  The teacher also (carry, carries) his books in a briefcase.  _____
7.  Frank (play, plays) the violin very well.                           _____
8.  Mary (play, plays) the piano very well.                            _____
9.  We (play, plays) tennis every afternoon.                          _____
10. Pedro and Henry also (play, plays) tennis every afternoon.  _____
11. George (does, do) this exercise very well.                       _____
12. Helen also (do, does) this exercise very well.                   _____
13. I always (try, tries) to come to school on time.               _____
14. You always (try, tries) to come to school on time.           _____
15. William also (try, tries) to come to school on time.         _____
16. I (want, wants) to learn English.                                      _____
17. John also (want, wants) to learn English.                       _____
18. Mr. and Mrs. Lecompte (go, goes) to the<br>    movies very often.                                                            _____
19. Mr. Lecompte (teach, teaches) English and French.        _____
20. The nurse (watch, watches) the patients.                        _____

9

*Change the sentences below to begin with* he *or* she. *Be sure to use the correct form of the verb.*

1.  I study English every day.                         *He studies*
2.  I like to study English.                           *She likes*
3.  I live in Miami.                                    _____
4.  I am a good student.                                _____
5.  I want to learn English well.                       _____
6.  I teach English.                                    _____
7.  I am very busy today.                                _____
8.  I go to the movies very often.                       _____
9.  I do these exercises every day.                      _____
10.  I see Mr. Ryan on the bus every day.                 _____
11.  I am a careful student.                              _____
12.  I carry a briefcase to class every day.              _____
13.  I have English lessons every day.                    _____
14.  I study English with Mr. Cruz.                       _____
15.  I play tennis very often.                            _____
16.  I try to come to school on time.                     _____
17.  I eat lunch in the cafeteria every day.              _____
18.  I try to speak English well.                         _____
19.  I study very hard.                                   _____
20.  I pass Mr. Fields on the street every day.           _____
21.  I go to school with John.                            _____
22.  I have two brothers.                                 _____

*Nouns that end in* y *form their plurals in two ways:*

| | |
|---|---|
| **a.** | **if a vowel precedes the** y, **add** s **to make the plural** |
| | key-keys   toy-toys   tray-trays |
| **b.** | **if a consonant precedes the** y, **change the** y **to** i **and add** es. |
| | city-cities   lady-ladies   country-countries |

*Most nouns that end in* f *or* fe *change their endings in the plural to* ves.

| half-halves   wife-wives   knife-knives |
|---|

*Nouns ending in* o *and preceded by a consonant form the plural by adding* es.

| potato-potatoes   hero-heroes |
|---|

*Some nouns have irregular plurals. These plurals must be memorized.*

| man-men | mouse-mice | foot-feet |
|---|---|---|
| woman-women | child-children | tooth-teeth |

*Write the plural form of the following words.*

| | | | | | |
|---|---|---|---|---|---|
| 1. | book | *books* | 15. | notebook | _____ |
| 2. | box | *boxes* | 16. | match | _____ |
| 3. | class | _____ | 17. | tail | _____ |
| 4. | brother | _____ | 18. | eye | _____ |
| 5. | friend | _____ | 19. | nose | _____ |
| 6. | cousin | _____ | 20. | dress | _____ |
| 7. | watch | _____ | 21. | woman | _____ |
| 8. | cafeteria | _____ | 22. | lunch | _____ |
| 9. | door | _____ | 23. | student | _____ |
| 10. | window | _____ | 24. | sister | _____ |
| 11. | wish | _____ | 25. | hat | _____ |
| 12. | teacher | _____ | 26. | man | _____ |
| 13. | pencil | _____ | 27. | coat | _____ |
| 14. | pen | _____ | 28. | tooth | _____ |

*Change the italicized word from singular to plural. Then make the necessary change in the form of the verb.*

1.  The *book* is on the desk.                          *The books are* _____
2.  The *man* speaks English well.                      _____
3.  The *boy* plays in the park.                        _____
4.  The *child* plays with the dog.                     _____
5.  The *mouse* runs into the hole.                     _____
6.  The *cat* runs after the mouse.                     _____
7.  *He* speaks English well.                           _____
8.  *I* play tennis every afternoon.                    _____
9.  *She* goes to school on the bus.                    _____
10. The *bus* arrives on time.                          _____
11. The *class* begins at one o'clock.                  _____
12. The *woman* is in the store.                        _____
13. The *dish* is on the table.                         _____
14. The *dress* is pretty.                              _____
15. The *pencil* is on the desk.                        _____
16. The *train* leaves at eight o'clock.                _____
17. The *watch* runs well.                              _____
18. The *box* is yellow.                                _____
19. The *church* is very large.                         _____
20. The *class* ends at two o'clock.                    _____
21. The *bus* is full.                                  _____
22. The *child* is sick.                                _____
23. The *woman* is busy.                                _____
24. The *man* is also busy.                             _____

# 13  Possessive adjectives

| | |
|---|---|
| my | our |
| your | your |
| his | their |
| her | |
| its | |
| I enjoy *my* new stereo. | They eat *their* breakfast at seven o'clock. |
| He washes *his* car. | We leave *our* home very early. |

*Write the correct possessive adjective in the blanks.*

1.  The boy walks to _____ chair.                                    *his*
2.  The girl walks to _____ chair.                              _____
3.  I walk to _____ chair.                                      _____
4.  We study _____ lessons every night.                         _____
5.  I put _____ notebook on the desk.                           _____
6.  Mary likes _____ English class.                             _____
7.  We bring _____ homework to class.                           _____
8.  The boys bring _____ homework to class.                     _____
9.  The girls bring _____ homework to class.                    _____
10. Our teacher, Mr. Roth comes to school in _____ car.         _____
11. John studies English in _____ room.                        _____
12. I study in _____ room.                                     _____
13. The dog chases _____ tail.                                 _____
14. The cat eats _____ dinner.                                 _____
15. I often look at _____ watch during the lesson.             _____
16. Ms. Megerian, our teacher, is pleased with _____
    work.                                                        _____
17. Many of the students look at _____ watches during
    the test.                                                    _____
18. You write many words in _____ notebooks every day.         _____
19. Grace always writes many words in _____ notebook.          _____

# 14 There is, there are

**We use** there is **with singular nouns; we use** there are **with plural nouns.**

| | |
|---|---|
| *There is* a book on the table. | *There are* two books on the table. |
| *There is* a woman in the office. | *There are* some women in the office. |

*Select the correct form. Write your answers in the blanks.*

1.  There (is, are) a magazine on the chair.               *is*
2.  There (is, are) two men in the office.            _____
3.  There (is, are) many children in the park.       _____
4.  There (is, are) many people on the bus.          _____
5.  There (is, are) a man at the door.              _____
6.  There (is, are) seven days in a week.           _____
7.  There (is, are) twelve months in a year.        _____
8.  There (is, are) a rug on the floor.             _____
9.  There (is, are) two windows in this room.       _____
10. There (is, are) many students in our class.      _____
11. There (is, are) many English classes in our school. _____
12. There (is, are) only one chair in this room.      _____
13. There (is, are) several pictures on the wall.     _____
14. There (is, are) only one cloud in the sky.       _____
15. There (is, are) two dishes on the table.        _____
16. There (is, are) many churches in this city.      _____
17. There (is, are) two women in Ms. Miller's office. _____
18. There (is, are) a letter for you.               _____
19. There (is, are) a goldfish in the pond.         _____
20. There (is, are) many new words in this lesson.    _____
21. There (is, are) a new student in our class.       _____
22. There (is, are) a visitor here for you.          _____

**Form the negative of** there is **and** there are **by placing** not **after the verb. The contracted forms** isn't **and** aren't **are generally used.**

| | |
|---|---|
| *There is* a good program on TV. | *There is not* a good program on TV. |
| | *There isn't* a good program on TV. |
| *There are* many museums to visit. | *There are not* many museums to visit. |
| | *There aren't* many museums to visit. |

*Change to the negative form. Use the contracted forms.*

1. There are many chairs in this room.      *aren't*
2. There is a radio in each room.      _____
3. There is a police officer on the corner.      _____
4. There are many offices in that building.      _____
5. There are many new students in our class.      _____
6. There are many children in the park.      _____
7. There is a computer in each room.      _____
8. There are many magazines on the desk.      _____
9. There is a window in the room.      _____
10. There are two doors in the room.      _____
11. There are many churches in this city.      _____
12. There is a rug on the floor.      _____
13. There are two people in the office.      _____
14. There is a letter here for you.      _____
15. There are many clouds in the sky.      _____
16. There are many new words in this lesson.      _____
17. There is a mouse in this room.      _____
18. There is one girl in our class.      _____
19. There are many exercises in this lesson.      _____
20. There is a library in this building.      _____
21. There are two telephones in the office.      _____
22. There is a map in our classroom.      _____

# 16  *There is, there are:* question form

**Form the questions with** there is **and** there are **by placing the verb before** there.

| | |
|---|---|
| *There is* a clock on the wall. | *Is there* a clock on the wall? |
| *There are* four cups of coffee on the table. | *Are there* four cups of coffee on the table? |

*Change to the question form. Write the verb and* there *in the blanks.*

1.  There is a police officer on the corner.          *Is there*
2.  There are many students in our class.          _____
3.  There is a clock in each classroom.          _____
4.  There is a window in each room.          _____
5.  There is a letter here for you.          _____
6.  There are many birds in the tree.          _____
7.  There are several fruits in the salad.          _____
8.  There is a library in this building.          _____
9.  There is a world map in my classroom.          _____
10.  There are two telephones in the office.          _____
11.  There is a hole in the wall.          _____
12.  There are many museums in this city.          _____
13.  There is a rug on the floor.          _____
14.  There are many flowers in the garden.          _____
15.  There are several new magazines here.          _____
16.  There is a radio in every room.          _____
17.  There is only one desk in the room.          _____
18.  There are only two mugs on the table.          _____
19.  There are many English classes in our school.          _____
20.  There are twelve inches in a foot.          _____
21.  There is only one person on the bus.          _____
22.  There are several pictures on the wall.          _____

**A *changes to* an *before any word beginning with a vowel sound.*
*In some English words beginning with* h, *the* h *is not pronounced.*
An *is used before these words.***

| | |
|---|---|
| a book | an apple |
| a happy person | an honest person |

*Use* a *or* an *before the following words.*

| | | | | | |
|---|---|---|---|---|---|
| 1. | *a* | New Yorker | 23. | _____ | easy exercise |
| 2. | *an* | Englishman | 24. | _____ | difficult exercise |
| 3. | _____ | German | 25. | _____ | honest man |
| 4. | _____ | book | 26. | _____ | big house |
| 5. | _____ | apple | 27. | _____ | old house |
| 6. | _____ | student | 28. | _____ | important lesson |
| 7. | _____ | umbrella | 29. | _____ | unimportant lesson |
| 8. | _____ | banana | 30. | _____ | good lesson |
| 9. | _____ | orange | 31. | _____ | bad lesson |
| 10. | _____ | horse | 32. | _____ | interesting lesson |
| 11. | _____ | elephant | 33. | _____ | unfair lesson |
| 12. | _____ | egg | 34. | _____ | easy lesson |
| 13. | _____ | argument | 35. | _____ | very easy lesson |
| 14. | _____ | month | 36. | _____ | late class |
| 15. | _____ | hour | 37. | _____ | early class |
| 16. | _____ | article | 38. | _____ | very early class |
| 17. | _____ | friend | 39. | _____ | excellent teacher |
| 18. | _____ | idea | 40. | _____ | cheap car |
| 19. | _____ | house | 41. | _____ | expensive car |
| 20. | _____ | car | 42. | _____ | nice meal |
| 21. | _____ | automobile | 43. | _____ | English book |
| 22. | _____ | island | 44. | _____ | French book |

**In English** this **and** that **are used both as pronouns and as adjectives without any change in form.** This **indicates something is near us;** that **indicates it is at a distance.**

| | |
|---|---|
| *This* cup is in front of me. | *That* cup is on the other side of the table. |
| *This* is a crystal vase. | *That* is a plain glass vase. |

**The plural of** this **is** these; **the plural of** that **is** those.

| | |
|---|---|
| *These* cups are in front of me. | *Those* cups are on the other side of the table. |
| *These* are porcelain plates. | *Those* are ironstone plates. |

*Change the italicized word or words to the plural form and write them and the verb in the blanks. Other changes in the rest of the sentence may be necessary.*

1.  *This book* is new.     *These books are*
2.  *That car* belongs to Mr. Gomez.     *Those cars belong*
3.  *That man* in the office is very competent. _____
4.  *This apple* is very good. _____
5.  *This exercise* is very difficult. _____
6.  *That pocketbook* on the table belongs to Mary. _____
7.  *This lesson* is very interesting. _____
8.  *This* is an interesting lesson. _____
9.  *That automobile* belongs to my father. _____
10.  *That* is my father's car. _____
11.  *That window* over there is open. _____
12.  *That* is the office of the vice president. _____
13.  *This letter* is for you. _____
14.  *That letter* is for Mr. Levine. _____
15.  *That house* near the corner is very old. _____
16.  *This umbrella* belongs to Adela. _____
17.  *This exercise* is very easy for me. _____
18.  *This* is an easy exercise for me. _____
19.  *That* is my hat. _____
20.  *That hat* belongs to me. _____

*Select the correct form. Write your answers in the blanks.*

1. Kenji (is, are) a good student.          *is*
2. (This, These) books belong to Helen.       _____
3. Henry and she (is, are) good friends.       _____
4. He (have, has) many friends in our class.       _____
5. I (don't have, doesn't have) a good pen.       _____
6. John (speak, speaks) English well.       _____
7. I (come, comes) to school by bus.       _____
8. There are two (church, churches) on this street.       _____
9. In autumn the (leafs, leaves) fall from the trees.       _____
10. (Tomatos, Tomatoes) are my favorite vegetable.       _____
11. (Do, Does) Helen have a new hat?       _____
12. The dog chases (its, it's) tail.       _____
13. There (is, are) seven days in a week.       _____
14. There (isn't, aren't) a window in the room.       _____
15. This is (a, an) English book.       _____
16. Mr. Smith is (a, an) old friend.       _____
17. I spend (a, an) hour on my homework every day.       _____
18. (That, Those) magazines belong to Helen.       _____
19. Mr. Smith (teach, teaches) English and French.       _____
20. Marie always (try, tries) to come to school on time.       _____
21. You and George (is, are) good friends.       _____
22. Grace and Carmen (has, have) many classes in this building.       _____
23. There (is, are) nobody in the office.       _____
24. This is (a, an) difficult exercise.       _____
25. He is (a, an) honest man.       _____

*The imperative form is used for a command or request. The subject* you *is understood but not expressed.*

| | |
|---|---|
| Come before seven o'clock. | (You) come before seven o'clock. |
| Wait for me here. | (You) wait for me here. |

*The negative of the imperative uses* don't.

| | |
|---|---|
| *Don't* stand out in the rain. | *Don't* eat between meals. |

*We use* please *at the beginning or end of imperatives to make them more polite.*

| | |
|---|---|
| Please sit down. | Wait for me here, please. |

*Change these imperative sentences to the negative form.*

1. Write your exercises in pencil.   *Don't write*.
2. Come back at two o'clock.   _____
3. Sit in that chair.   _____
4. Open the window.   _____
5. Close the door.   _____
6. Ask Mr. Oguri to come in.   _____
7. Take the next bus.   _____
8. Wait on that corner.   _____
9. Put your books there on that chair.   _____
10. Hang your coat on that hanger.   _____
11. Study the next lesson.   _____
12. Write all the exercises in this lesson.   _____
13. Help John with his lesson.   _____
14. Speak Spanish to the new girl.   _____
15. Use the new words in this lesson.   _____
16. Give this to Mr. Smith.   _____
17. Sit in the sun.   _____
18. Drive fast.   _____
19. Tell Valentina to wait for us.   _____
20. Look out the window.   _____

| Subject | Object | Subject | Object |
|---------|--------|---------|--------|
| I | me | we | us |
| you | you | you | you |
| he | him | they | them |
| she | her | | |
| it | it | | |

**Object pronouns are used as direct objects, indirect objects, and objects of prepositions.**

I know *her* very well.

She gives *us* a lot of help.

They gave it to *him*.

*Select the correct form. Write your answer in the blanks.*

1. I see (he, him) on the bus every day.                                   *him*
2. He sits near (I, me) in class.                                          _____
3. I go with (she, her) to the movies very often.                          _____
4. We often see (they, them) at school.                                    _____
5. I like (she, her) very much.                                            _____
6. I know both (he, him) and his brother very well.                        _____
7. He sits near (we, us) at the lesson.                                    _____
8. Don't speak to (they, them) in Spanish.                                 _____
9. I often go with (they, them) to the movies.                             _____ _ _
10. He often helps (I, me) with my lessons.                                _____
11. She writes many letters to (he, him).                                  _____
12. Don't lend money to (she, her).                                        _____
13. Mr. Prins teaches (we, us) English.                                    _____
14. He gives many presents to (she, her).                                  _____
15. Please explain this exercise to (me, I).                               _____
16. Please give this book to (him, he).                                    _____
17. Don't go with (them, they) to the movie tonight.                       _____
18. The teacher always explains the lesson to (we, us).                    _____
19. He wants to talk with (me, I).                                         _____
20. I like (they, them) very much.                                         _____
21. He seldom speaks to (us, we).                                          _____

# 22   Object pronouns 2

*Change the italicized word or words to the correct object pronouns.*

1. I see *John* on the bus every morning.                           *him*
2. I often go to the movies with *Mary* .                           _____
3. I like *Nelson and Henry* very much.                             _____
4. He never speaks to *Mary and me*.                               _____
5. I also like *Mary and Helen* very much.                         _____
6. She writes many letters to *her sister*.                         _____
7. I sit near *Max and his brother*.                               _____
8. I see *Helen* in the cafeteria every day.                       _____
9. I understand *my teacher, Mr. Chandra*, very well.              _____
10. He gives *his son* much money.                                _____
11. She always speaks to *her daughter* in Spanish.               _____
12. He sends *his sister and you* many presents.                  _____
13. John writes many letters to *his aunt*.                       _____
14. I write many letters to *my uncle*.                           _____
15. I sit near *Mary and Helen* at the lesson.                    _____
16. Helen sits near *Franco and George*.                          _____
17. She says that she sees *you and Karen* on the bus
    every morning.                                                _____
18. I often see *those boys* in the cafeteria.                    _____
19. I know both *Henry and his brother* very well.                _____
20. All the girls like *their teacher, Ms. Lee*, very well.       _____
21. I often go to the movies with *my parents*.                   _____

### days, months, seasons

**The days of the week are** Sunday, Monday, Tuesday, Wednesday, Thursday, Friday, **and** Saturday.

**The months of the year are** January, February, March, April, May, June, July, August, September, October, November, **and** December.

**The four seasons of the year are** spring, summer, autumn (fall), **and** winter.

*Write the correct answers in the blanks.*

1. The first month of the year is _____ .                    *January*
2. The second month of the year is _____ .                   _____
3. The third month of the year is _____ .                    _____
4. The last month of the year is _____ .                     _____
5. The month of June comes before the month of _____ .       _____
6. The month of September comes before the month of _____ .  _____
7. The month of May comes after the month of _____ .         _____
8. The month of August comes after the month of _____ .      _____
9. In the United States, elections take place during the month of _____ .   _____
10. In the United States, the weather during the months of July and August is generally very _____ .   _____
11. In the United States, the weather during the months of January and February is generally _____ .   _____
12. The first day of the week is _____ .                     _____
13. The second day of the week is _____ .                    _____
14. The last day of the week is _____ .                      _____
15. Monday comes before _____ .                              _____
16. Thursday comes before _____ .                            _____
17. Wednesday comes after _____ .                            _____

| | |
|---|---|
| I was | we were |
| you were | you were |
| he was | they were |
| she was | |
| it was | |

*Change to the past tense; write the correct form of the verb in the blanks.*

1.  He *is* a good student.                    *was*
2.  I *am* also a good student.              _____
3.  John *is* in my class.                        _____
4.  We *are* good friends.                      _____
5.  Helen and Roger *are* in the same class.   _____
6.  The door *is* open.                          _____
7.  The windows and doors *are* open.       _____
8.  The book *is* on the table.                _____
9.  I *am* very hungry.                          _____
10. Mary and Jennifer *are* students.       _____
11. Ms. Lopez *is* our teacher.               _____
12. This *is* an easy exercise.                _____
13. The weather *is* good.                      _____
14. Both doors *are* closed.                    _____
15. This lesson *is* easy.                        _____
16. You and Eleni *are* good friends.       _____
17. Yoshiko and I *are* also good friends.  _____
18. You *are* a good student.                  _____
19. There *is* someone at the door.          _____
20. There *are* many students in our class. _____
21. There *is* a magazine on this desk.      _____

# 25 Regular verbs: past tense

**The past tense of regular verbs is formed by adding** ed **to the simple form of the verb.**

> work-worked

**Notice the formation of the past tense with these regular verbs.**

> live-lived    study-studied

**When the simple form of the verb ends in** y **preceded by a consonant, the** y **is changed to** i **before adding** ed.

> study-*studied*    marry-*married*

**Compare with a similar change in the third person singular of the present tense.**

> study-*studies*    marry-*marries*

*Change the verb of each sentence to the past tense.*

1. We always *walk* to school.          *walked*
2. He *arrives* at school on time every day.          _____
3. Our lesson *ends* at two o'clock.          _____
4. He *lives* in Miami.          _____
5. They *study* in our class.          _____
6. We *finish* our lessons at three o'clock.          _____
7. I *like* chess a lot.          _____
8. Helen *answers* all of the teacher's questions.          _____
9. We *walk* through the park every morning.          _____
10. The dog *follows* the boy everywhere.          _____
11. I *need* a new book.          _____
12. We always *wait* for her on this corner.          _____
13. He *wants* a new car.          _____
14. We *learn* many new words in this class.          _____
15. I *use* my new pen in every class.          _____
16. We *listen* to the radio every night.          _____
17. My parents *watch* television every night.          _____

**If the simple form of a verb ends in** t **or** d, **the** ed **in the past tense is pronounced as a separate syllable.**

| count-count-ed | need-need-ed |

**If the simple form does not end in** t **or** d, **then the** ed **in the past tense is not pronounced as a separate syllable. It takes the sound of** d **or** t.

| show-showed (pronounced *d*) | walk-walked (pronounced *t*) |

*Pronounce the following past tense forms. Then write the number 1 or 2 to show whether the word is pronounced as a word of one syllable or as a word of two syllables.*

| | | | | | |
|---|---|---|---|---|---|
| 1. | ended | **2** | 21. | mended | _____ |
| 2. | filled | **1** | 22. | picked | _____ |
| 3. | counted | _____ | 23. | parted | _____ |
| 4. | rented | _____ | 24. | looked | _____ |
| 5. | needed | _____ | 25. | lived | _____ |
| 6. | showed | _____ | 26. | liked | _____ |
| 7. | planted | _____ | 27. | lasted | _____ |
| 8. | worked | _____ | 28. | closed | _____ |
| 9. | washed | _____ | 29. | changed | _____ |
| 10. | wanted | _____ | 30. | landed | _____ |
| 11. | waited | _____ | 31. | used | _____ |
| 12. | walked | _____ | 32. | mailed | _____ |
| 13. | stopped | _____ | 33. | handed | _____ |
| 14. | spelled | _____ | 34. | crossed | _____ |
| 15. | smoked | _____ | 35. | pulled | _____ |
| 16. | fainted | _____ | 36. | earned | _____ |
| 17. | pointed | _____ | 37. | painted | _____ |
| 18. | asked | _____ | 38. | boiled | _____ |
| 19. | danced | _____ | 39. | burned | _____ |
| 20. | talked | _____ | 40. | touched | _____ |

**Many verbs in English have special past tense forms. Study and memorize these verbs. They are the same in all three persons, both singular and plural.**

| buy | bought | get | got | sit | sat |
|-----|--------|-----|-----|-----|-----|
| come | came | have (has) | had | spin | spun |
| drink | drank | put | put | speak | spoke |
| eat | ate | read | read | write | wrote |

| I sat | we sat |
|-------|--------|
| you sat | you sat |
| he sat | they sat |
| she sat | |
| it sat | |

*Change the following sentences to the past tense.*

1. She writes many letters.     *wrote*
2. He buys many books. _____
3. I read the *New York Times*. _____
4. She drinks milk with her meals. _____
5. He has many friends. _____
6. Sonia sits in this seat. _____
7. He eats lunch in the cafeteria. _____
8. I get up early. _____
9. He speaks English well. _____
10. He puts his books on this table. _____
11. She comes to school by bus. _____
12. They have a new car. _____
13. She and Tomiko drink coffee with their lunch. _____
14. I always sit near the window. _____
15. They speak Spanish. _____
16. He gets up at ten o'clock. _____
17. We eat dinner at home. _____
18. The washing machine spins the clothes dry. _____
19. I buy all my books in the school bookstore. _____
20. We write our exercises in the workbook. _____

## mistakes of fact 1

**The items in boldface are mistakes. Change them to make the facts correct, and write your answers in the blanks.**

1.  The first month of the year is **February**.    *January*
2.  The last month of the year is **November**.    _____
3.  The next-to-the-last month of the year is **October**.    _____
4.  September comes **after** October.    _____
5.  July comes **before** June.    _____
6.  There are **eight** days in a week.    _____
7.  The first day of the week is **Tuesday**.    _____
8.  The last day of the week is **Friday**.    _____
9.  Monday comes **after** Tuesday.    _____
10. Friday comes **before** Thursday.    _____
11. The month of February usually has **twenty-nine** days.    _____
12. The four seasons of the year are spring, summer, autumn, and **Christmas**.    _____
13. In the United States, spring begins on **June** 21.    _____
14. In the United States, summer begins on **March** 21.    _____
15. The past tense of the irregular verb *to sit* is **set**.    _____
16. The past tense of the verb *to buy* is **buyed**.    _____
17. The plural form of the word *child* is **childs**.    _____
18. The plural form of the word *woman* is **womans**.    _____
19. There are **fifty** seconds in a minute.    _____
20. There are **seventy** minutes in an hour.    _____
21. The opposite of *tall* is **big**.    _____

*Write the opposites of the following words.*

| | | | | | |
|---|---|---|---|---|---|
| 1. | tall | *short* | 24. | bad | _____ |
| 2. | high | _____ | 25. | bring | _____ |
| 3. | in | _____ | 26. | down | _____ |
| 4. | good | _____ | 27. | asleep | _____ |
| 5. | yes | _____ | 28. | out | _____ |
| 6. | present | _____ | 29. | no | _____ |
| 7. | up | _____ | 30. | true | _____ |
| 8. | black | _____ | 31. | absent | _____ |
| 9. | many | _____ | 32. | white | _____ |
| 10. | before | _____ | 33. | few | _____ |
| 11. | easy | _____ | 34. | after | _____ |
| 12. | push | _____ | 35. | difficult | _____ |
| 13. | hot | _____ | 36. | pull | _____ |
| 14. | first | _____ | 37. | cold | _____ |
| 15. | big | _____ | 38. | cool | _____ |
| 16. | cheap | _____ | 39. | sit | _____ |
| 17. | sweet | _____ | 40. | last | _____ |
| 18. | early | _____ | 41. | little | _____ |
| 19. | warm | _____ | 42. | expensive | _____ |
| 20. | soft | _____ | 43. | sour | _____ |
| 21. | day | _____ | 44. | night | _____ |
| 22. | sell | _____ | 45. | stop | _____ |
| 23. | thick | _____ | 46. | buy | _____ |

*Write the correct prepositions in the blanks.*

1. People see _____ their eyes.      *with*
2. I always eat _____ the cafeteria.      _____
3. January comes _____ February.      _____
4. Every morning I leave home _____ eight o'clock.      _____
5. Sometimes I walk _____ work.      _____
6. I write all the new words _____ my notebook.      _____
7. I like to travel _____ plane.      _____
8. What is the opposite _____ the word *pull?*      _____
9. I arrive _____ work at nine o'clock.      _____
10. How many months are there _____ a year?      _____
11. January is the first month _____ the year.      _____
12. I was late _____ class yesterday.      _____
13. I always walk _____ school.      _____
14. There is a large map _____ the wall.      _____
15. She explained everything _____ me.      _____
16. April comes _____ March.      _____
17. I spoke _____ Carmen about that matter.      _____
18. John put the letter _____ an envelope.      _____
19. I get up _____ seven o'clock every morning.      _____
20. They always come to school _____ bus.      _____
21. I put the letter _____ the mailbox.      _____
22. Yesterday Andy paid my fare _____ the bus.      _____
23. I had only a sandwich _____ lunch.      _____
24. Don't write your exercises _____ pencil.      _____

*Select the correct form. Write your answers in the blanks.*

1. William and Mary (is, are) good dancers.     *are*
2. Helen (was, were) absent from class yesterday. _____
3. John (speak, speaks) English well. _____
4. Yesterday morning I (get, got) up very late. _____
5. I often see (they, them) in the cafeteria. _____
6. Don't lend money to (she, her). _____
7. There (isn't, aren't) one window in the room. _____
8. I spend (a, an) hour on my homework every day. _____
9. John sat down and (puts, put) his feet up on a chair. _____
10. There (was, were) nobody in the office. _____
11. (Does, Do) she have many friends in the class? _____
12. He teaches (we, us) English. _____
13. Both doors (were, was) closed. _____
14. Last night we stayed at home and (watch, watched) television. _____
15. John was absent (in, from) the lesson yesterday. _____
16. They (studies, study) English every day. _____
17. How many English books (does, do) you have? _____
18. (Was, Were) you at the lesson yesterday? _____
19. He is (a, an) very old man. _____
20. Is John (a, an) excellent athlete? _____
21. My father usually (get, gets) up early every morning. _____
22. What color (is, are) your shoes? _____
23. She is (a, an) honest woman. _____
24. Last night we (eat, ate) dinner at home. _____

# 32  Review: past tense 1

*Change the following verbs to the past tense.*

1. We walk through the park every day.  *walked*
2. He is a good student.  _____
3. He drinks coffee with all his meals.  _____
4. They come to school by bus.  _____
5. He needs a new suit.  _____
6. He talks to us in English.  _____
7. We are good students.  _____
8. He has many friends here.  _____
9. They have a new car.  _____
10. He speaks Spanish well.  _____
11. She and I are students in the same class.  _____
12. He reads the newspaper at breakfast.  _____
13. I buy all my clothes in that store.  _____
14. He smokes a lot.  _____
15. We learn many new words.  _____
16. The teacher asks us many questions.  _____
17. Our lesson ends at two o'clock.  _____
18. The weather is good.  _____
19. Both windows are closed.  _____
20. There is nobody at home.  _____
21. He follows his brother everywhere.  _____

# 33 Review: past tense 2

*Change the following verbs to the present tense.*

1. He often came to see us.                                  *comes*
2. They had many friends in our class.          _____
3. I bought all my books in the school bookstore.  _____
4. They usually spoke English with us.          _____
5. Susan read a good novel.                         _____
6. We always ate lunch in the cafeteria.         _____
7. They were good students.                          _____
8. She was my teacher.                                  _____
9. I waited on the corner for them.               _____
10. He asked us for directions.                       _____
11. I got up very early.                                   _____
12. She wrote many letters to me.                  _____
13. He put his books on this desk.                   _____
14. He needed more lessons.                           _____
15. The bus stopped on this corner.               _____
16. We were very busy.                                    _____
17. He liked to swim.                                      _____
18. She wanted to learn English.                    _____
19. It was an easy exercise.                            _____
20. There were many students absent.            _____
21. They came to school on time.                    _____

# 34  Auxiliary verbs: negative form

**Verbs like** can, may, should, **and** must **are auxiliary verbs. We form the negative of an auxiliary verb by placing** not **after it.** Can + not **is a special case. It is always written as one word.**

| | |
|---|---|
| You must go there early. | You *must not* go there early. |
| We can speak English. | We *cannot* speak English. |

*Change to the negative form. Write the complete verb in the blanks.*

1. She should work late.          *should not work*
2. He should speak German in this class.    _____
3. You may smoke here.           _____
4. They may be very busy.          _____
5. He must see her.            _____
6. I can telephone him later.         _____
7. You should tell her all about it.       _____
8. She must go today.           _____
9. She can play the piano well.        _____
10. You may open the window.        _____
11. They may be back before noon.       _____
12. He can do all of these exercises well.     _____
13. Arturo may go to the party with us.      _____
14. You may wait here.           _____
15. They can meet us later.         _____
16. He should sit near the window.       _____
17. We must tell John about it.        _____
18. He can go with us to the movies.      _____
19. You may sit here beside John.       _____
20. We must do that again.         _____

**To form a question with an auxiliary verb, place the auxiliary verb before the subject.**

| | |
|---|---|
| *We can* speak several languages. | *Can we* speak several languages? |
| *They may* go with you. | *May they* go with you? |

*Change to the question form. Write the complete verb and subject in the blanks.*

1. She can speak French well.             *Can she speak*
2. He should wait on that corner.         _____
3. They may smoke here.                   _____
4. Sam can meet you at two o'clock.       _____
5. He must go out of town.                _____
6. She should tell Helen about it.        _____
7. She can go with us tonight.            _____
8. He may wait in Mr. Smith's office.     _____
9. We must explain it to him.             _____
10. Toby may wait in his office.          _____
11. They may sit here.                    _____
12. You should stay at home.              _____
13. He can meet us after dinner.          _____
14. He can swim very well.                _____
15. You must write him a letter.          _____
16. She can attend class tomorrow.        _____
17. He can play the violin well.          _____
18. They can speak Spanish well.          _____
19. Ricardo can understand everything he says.  _____
20. She can do all these exercises well.  _____

## 36 Simple present tense:

### negative form

**To form the negative of the simple present tense, place** do not **or** does not **before the verb. We normally use the contracted forms** don't **and** doesn't.

| | |
|---|---|
| I do not drive. (I don't drive.) | We do not drive. |
| You do not drive. (You don't drive.) | (We don't drive.) |
| He does not drive. (He doesn't drive.) | You do not drive. |
| She does not drive. (She doesn't drive.) | (You don't drive.) |
| It does not drive. (It doesn't drive.) | They do not drive. |
| | (They don't drive.) |

**Note that after** does not (doesn't), **the verb does not have the** s **of the third person singular affirmative statement.**

*Change to the negative form. Write both the full form and the contracted form.*

1. He studies in our class.      *does not study*    *doesn't study*
2. They go to the movies every night. _____ _____
3. She comes to school by bus. _____ _____
4. I know him very well. _____ _____
5. It rains very often during the month of April. _____ _____
6. The dog runs after the cat. _____ _____
7. Our class begins at eight o'clock. _____ _____
8. It ends at ten o'clock. _____ _____
9. The buses stop on this corner. _____ _____
10. We write many letters. _____ _____
11. She speaks English well. _____ _____
12. You walk to work every day. _____ _____
13. They like to study English. _____ _____
14. Helen lives in Chicago. _____ _____
15. He works on Sunday. _____ _____
16. I go to school by bus. _____ _____
17. I arrive at school on time. _____ _____
18. We need more practice in English. _____ _____
19. I understand him very well. _____ _____
20. She gets up early every morning. _____ _____

**Simple present tense:**

## question form 1

**Form questions in the simple present tense by placing** do **or** does **before the subject.**

| | |
|---|---|
| Do I work? | Do we work? |
| Do you work? | Do you work? |
| Does he work? | Do they work? |
| Does she work? | |
| Does it work? | |

*Change to the question form. Write the complete verb and subject.*

1.  He comes to school by bus.      *Does he come*
2.  They speak Spanish well.      _____
3.  He gets up early every morning.      _____
4.  The Browns eat dinner at home.      _____
5.  They like Mexican food.      _____
6.  He wants more time.      _____
7.  The students prefer a take-home exam.      _____
8.  He talks to us in English.      _____
9.  They live near the corner.      _____
10. He takes his car to work every day.      _____
11. John smokes too much.      _____
12. She dances well.      _____
13. They know him very well.      _____
14. You understand everything he says.      _____
15. They get up early every morning.      _____
16. He reads a lot of computer magazines.      _____
17. We want a new car.      _____
18. They come to class early.      _____
19. Mary arrives late for appointments.      _____
20. It rains very often during this month.      _____
21. He eats lunch in the cafeteria.      _____
22. They sell newspapers there.      _____

## question form 2

Do **or** does **is used with question words like** why, where, when, what time, how, **and** how much.

> *Where does* Joseph live?
>
> *When do* you leave for vacation?
>
> *How much does* it cost?
>
> *What time do* you have?

*Write* do *or* does *in the blanks.*

1. Where _____ Helen work?                                       *does*
2. Where _____ you live? _____
3. What time _____ your lesson begin? _____
4. What time _____ you arrive at school every day? _____
5. How well _____ Mohammed speak English? _____
6. When _____ the next train arrive? _____
7. Why _____ they work so hard? _____
8. What time _____ you get up every morning? _____
9. Where _____ John eat lunch every day? _____
10. How much _____ it cost to go to Chicago by plane? _____
11. When _____ Mr. Pelli and Joe expect to return? _____
12. How often _____ it rain during the month of April? _____
13. Where _____ you eat dinner every night? _____
14. Why _____ John walk to school alone every day? _____
15. Where _____ he go after the lesson? _____
16. Where _____ Mercedes and her sister live? _____
17. How often _____ you go to the movies? _____
18. What language besides English _____ your
    teacher speak? _____
19. How _____ you feel today? _____
20. What time _____ you go to bed every night? _____
21. Why _____ Helen want to learn English? _____
22. How many hours _____ you sleep every night? _____

### past tense, negative form

**To form the negative of** to be **in the past tense, place** not **after the verb. Notice how the contractions are formed.**

| | | |
|---|---|---|
| I was not there. | (I wasn't there.) | We were not there. |
| You were not there. | (You weren't there.) | (We weren't there.) |
| He was not there. | (He wasn't there.) | You were not there. |
| She was not there. | (She wasn't there.) | (You weren't there.) |
| It was not there. | (It wasn't there.) | They were not there. |
| | | (They weren't there.) |

*Change to the negative form. Use the contractions* wasn't *and* weren't.

1.  John was in my class.                              *wasn't*
2.  We were very good friends.                         _____
3.  The door was open.                                 _____
4.  The lesson was easy.                               _____
5.  You and George were at the meeting.                _____
6.  There were many students absent from class.        _____
7.  There was a magazine on the desk.                  _____
8.  We were in the same class.                         _____
9.  They were cousins.                                 _____
10. The doors were closed.                             _____
11. I was very hungry.                                 _____
12. Ms. Rosas was our teacher.                         _____
13. The weather was very good.                         _____
14. They were Mexicans.                                _____
15. She was a good companion.                          _____
16. It was a very nice day.                            _____
17. They were in Europe all summer.                    _____
18. I was busy yesterday.                              _____
19. He was a tall man.                                 _____
20. We were dead tired.                                _____
21. It was a very cold day.                            _____
22. There were many interesting things in the article. _____

## 40  To be:

### past tense, question form

**To form questions in the past tense of** to be, **place the verb before the subject. In** there **and** to be **sentences, place the verb before** there.

| | |
|---|---|
| You were in Europe last year. | *Were you* in Europe last year? |
| It was a good movie. | *Was it* a good movie? |
| There was pie for dessert. | *Was there* pie for dessert? |

*Change to questions by placing the verb before the subject or* there.

1.  He was an old friend.                                   *Was he*
2.  They were busy all day long.                            _____
3.  He was a very intelligent person.                       _____
4.  There were many students absent from the lesson.        _____
5.  The windows were open.                                  _____
6.  The door was closed.                                    _____
7.  They were in Europe all summer.                         _____
8.  There was a radio on the table.                         _____
9.  We were both dead tired.                                _____
10. They are both North Americans.                          _____
11. We were in the army together.                           _____
12. The lesson was easy.                                    _____
13. The teacher was very angry.                             _____
14. He and she were tennis partners.                        _____
15. The exercises were difficult.                           _____
16. The woman was a stranger to me.                         _____
17. There was a letter for you on the table.                _____
18. It was a small dark object.                             _____
19. There were many dark clouds in the sky.                 _____
20. There was a large rug on the floor.                     _____
21. Angela was angry with him.                              _____
22. You were late for your lesson this morning.             _____

40

**To form the negative past tense of all verbs (except** to be**), place**
did not **before the simple form of the verb. The auxiliary** did **is
the same for all persons in the past tense. The contraction** didn't
**is generally used.**

| | | |
|---|---|---|
| I did not stop. | (I didn't stop.) | We did not stop. |
| You did not stop. | (You didn't stop.) | (We didn't stop.) |
| He did not stop. | (He didn't stop.) | You did not stop. |
| She did not stop. | (She didn't stop.) | (You didn't stop.) |
| It did not stop. | (It didn't stop.) | They did not stop. |
| | | (They didn't stop.) |

*Change to the negative form. Write the complete verb and subject
in the blanks. Use the contracted form of the auxiliary.*

1. He spoke to me about it yesterday.                        *He didn't speak*
2. She came to the lesson on time.                        _____
3. We ate lunch in the cafeteria.                        _____
4. I bought all my books in the bookstore.                        _____
5. The child drank all the milk.                        _____
6. She wanted new glasses.                        _____
7. He needed more lessons.                        _____
8. I waited for you on the corner.                        _____
9. He read the newspaper this morning.                        _____
10. We watched television last night.                        _____
11. He had many friends in the class.                        _____
12. He liked French movies.                        _____
13. She put all her books on the table.                        _____
14. I got up early this morning.                        _____
15. John came with me to the lesson.                        _____
16. He asked me several questions about it.                        _____
17. We learned many new words yesterday.                        _____
18. I wrote a letter to my sister.                        _____
19. The bus stopped on this corner.                        _____
20. We ate dinner at home.                        _____
21. She sat beside me on the bus.                        _____
22. She got very sick during the boat ride.                        _____

# 42 Past tense: question form

*Form the past tense question by placing* did *before the subject and by changing the verb to its simple form.*

| | |
|---|---|
| Did I go home? | Did we go home? |
| Did you go home? | Did you go home? |
| Did he go home? | Did they go home? |
| Did she go home? | |
| Did it go home? | |

*Change to the question form. Write the complete verb and subject in the blanks.*

1.   He spoke to me about it yesterday.                                   *Did he speak*

2.   She waited for us on the corner.                                      _____

3.   They wrote him several letters.                                       _____

4.   The bus stopped on this corner.                                       _____

5.   They had dinner with us last night.                                   _____

6.   She wanted to go with us.                                             _____

7.   He preferred to stay at home.                                         _____

8.   Monica knew him very well.                                            _____

9.   You got up very early this morning.                                   _____

10.  They came to school by bus.                                           _____

11.  Julio read about the accident in the newspaper last night. _____

12.  They lived near us.                                                   _____

13.  She spoke to them in Spanish.                                         _____

14.  We talked together for a long time.                                   _____

15.  He bought his car in Europe.                                          _____

16.  She put on her hat and coat.                                          _____

17.  It rained very hard last night.                                       _____

18.  He arrived late for the lesson.                                       _____

19.  She wrote him a letter from New York.                                 _____

20.  We ate dinner in a restaurant last night.                            _____

21.  They sat near her at the play.                                        _____

22.  The lesson ended at eight o'clock.                                    _____

*Write the correct prepositions in the blanks.*

1. Sometimes I walk _____ school.                                  *to*
2. Do you take sugar _____ your coffee?                            _____
3. The train for Chicago leaves _____ three o'clock.               _____
4. It arrives _____ Chicago at ten o'clock.                        _____
5. What did you have _____ lunch?                                  _____
6. Our class begins _____ nine o'clock.                            _____
7. I thanked him _____ the information.                            _____
8. I spoke to him _____ the phone yesterday.                       _____
9. Tell me all _____ your trip to Washington.                      _____
10. The teacher stands _____ the class.                            _____
11. There is a map on the wall just _____ the teacher's desk.  _____
12. February comes _____ March.                                    _____
13. July comes _____ June.                                         _____
14. *Tall* is the opposite _____ *short*.                          _____
15. They live in that house _____ the corner.                      _____
16. I was late _____ my lesson this morning.                       _____
17. John was absent _____ class yesterday.                         _____
18. He put the stamp _____ the envelope.                           _____
19. I like to travel _____ train.                                  _____
20. She often goes to the movies _____ us.                         _____
21. He asked me _____ a pencil.                                     _____
22. She asked me all _____ my trip to Chicago.                     _____
23. How many months are there _____ a year?                       _____
24. The dog jumped _____ the fence.                                _____

# 44 Irregular verbs: past tense 2

*Study and memorize the past tense forms of the following irregular verbs.*

| | | | | | |
|---|---|---|---|---|---|
| begin | began | go | went | see | saw |
| (it) costs | cost | hear | heard | sell | sold |
| fall | fell | know | knew | stand | stood |
| feel | felt | leave | left | tell | told |
| give | gave | ride | rode | understand | understood |

*Change the following sentences to the past tense.*

1. He goes to school in London.      *went*
2. I hear someone in the next room.      _____
3. She feels very well after her operation.      _____
4. We ride the bus to work.      _____
5. I see him on the street.      _____
6. The teacher tells us many interesting stories.      _____
7. Our lesson begins at eight o'clock.      _____
8. I know him very well.      _____
9. The train leaves at ten o'clock.      _____
10. This dress costs ten dollars.      _____
11. She gives me a lot of presents.      _____
12. They sell many different things in that store.      _____
13. Our teacher stands in front of the class.      _____
14. I understand him well.      _____
15. We see him in the cafeteria.      _____
16. People fall on the broken stones.      _____
17. He leaves home at eight o'clock.      _____
18. The movie begins at eight o'clock.      _____
19. We go to the movies on Wednesday night.      _____
20. She tells me the answers to all the exercises.      _____
21. We ride through the park on our bicycles.      _____
22. At the end of the school year, I sell all my books.      _____

# 45 Vocabulary review 1

*Select the correct answer and write it in the space provided.*

1. I see with my (ears, eyes, nose, mouth).       *eyes*

2. The past tense of the verb *to feel* is
(fall, full, felt, feels). _____

3. We buy stamps in a (restaurant, cafeteria,
post office, mailbox). _____

4. We pronounce the word *comb* to rhyme with
(come, thumb, home, some). _____

5. The next-to-the-last month of the year is
(January, February, November, December). _____

6. The opposite of *put on* is (put away, take off,
stop, begin). _____

7. Which one of these past tense forms do we pronounce
as a word of only one syllable: *counted, painted,
walked, wanted?* _____

8. We hear with our (eyes, ears, hands, nose). _____

9. Which of these do you pay on the bus: bill,
rent, fare, tax? _____

10. Which of these do you wear on your hands: tie, shirt,
gloves, socks? _____

11. The opposite of *push* is (open, close, put, pull). _____

12. In the United States, the weather during the months
of January and February is (warm, cold, hot, rainy). _____

13. We pronounce the word *these* to rhyme with (this,
nose, sneeze, police). _____

14. The opposite of *cheap* is (poor, expensive, rich, new). _____

15. Which letter of the word *answer* is silent
(not pronounced)? _____

16. Which letter of the word *walk* is silent (not pronounced)?_____

17. Which one of these meals do we eat in the morning:
breakfast, lunch, dinner, supper? _____

*Select the correct form. Write your answers in the blanks.*

1. (Did, Does) John go with you to the movie last night?    *Did*
2. Mary (get, gets) up every morning at seven o'clock.    _____
3. (This, These) books are new.    _____
4. Do people (see, sees) with their eyes or with their ears?    _____
5. What time (do, did) you get up this morning?    _____
6. Do you want (a, an) apple?    _____
7. This is (a, an) hot day.    _____
8. She is (a, an) honest person.    _____
9. Where (you went, did you go) yesterday after class?    _____
10. Mary likes (speak, to speak) English with the teacher.    _____
11. How many books does Esther (have, has)?    _____
12. There (is, are) two men in Ms. Garcia's office.    _____
13. Henry and Olga (was, were) not in class yesterday.    _____
14. I (eat, ate) lunch with Ali yesterday.    _____
15. Yesterday I (get, got) up at six o'clock.    _____
16. How many days (is, are) there in a week?    _____
17. They (go, goes) to the movies almost every night.    _____
18. I saw (she, her) in the cafeteria yesterday.    _____
19. She cannot (speak, to speak) English well.    _____
20. I often meet (they, them) on the street.    _____
21. They (do, does) not study in our class.    _____
22. Mr. and Mrs. Chin (wasn't, weren't) at the meeting last night.    _____
23. (Do, Did) you get to the class on time this morning?    _____
24. I (come, came) home very late last night.    _____

### past tense, negative form

**To form the negative of** to have **in the past tense, place** did not **before the simple form of the verb. The contraction** didn't **is generally used.**

| | |
|---|---|
| I had a good time. | I *did not (didn't)* have a good time. |
| She had an accident. | She *did not (didn't)* have an accident. |

*Change the affirmative sentences to the negative form. Change the negative sentences to the affirmative form. Use the negative contraction.*

1. Helen had many friends in our class.      *didn't have*
2. I didn't have a Sony TV before this one.      *had*
3. We had three English teachers last year. _____
4. They had a new car. _____
5. We had a good time at the party last night. _____
6. I had an English lesson yesterday morning. _____
7. They didn't have their vacation in June. _____
8. Bill had a good time skiing. _____
9. She had two dogs and a cat. _____
10. We had many new words to learn today. _____
11. Judith didn't have new glasses on. _____
12. You had new contact lenses. _____
13. We had our English class in Room 203. _____
14. I didn't have lunch in the cafeteria today. _____
15. We had dinner in a restaurant last night. _____
16. I didn't have a bad cold. _____
17. Juan had a headache. _____
18. We had a nice vacation. _____
19. They had many friends in Panama. _____
20. That dog had a lot of fleas. _____
21. The teacher didn't have a large class. _____
22. This book had international success. _____

## past tense, question form

**To form the question of** to have **in the past tense, place** did **before the subject. The simple form of the verb follows the subject.**

| | |
|---|---|
| We had enough time. | *Did we have* enough time? |
| They had good grades. | *Did they* have good grades? |
| Joan had a good job offer. | *Did Joan have* a good job offer? |

*Change to the question form. Use* did, *the subject, and the simple form of* to have.

1.  He had many friends here.      *Did he have* _____

2.  They had a good time at the dance last night. _____

3.  You had a good meal in that restaurant. _____

4.  She had two cousins in our school. _____

5.  The teacher had a good group of students. _____

6.  You had a headache. _____

7.  We had our English class at ten o'clock. _____

8.  She had lunch with Helen yesterday. _____

9.  They had a new television set. _____

10.  They had a very good time in Mexico last summer. _____

11.  She had a bad cold. _____

12.  Your father had a store in town. _____

13.  Helen had two brothers in the army. _____

14.  He had his vacation in June this year. _____

15.  Last year, he had his vacation in August. _____

16.  This room had a map on the wall before. _____

17.  The movie had a good ending. _____

18.  The child had both a cat and a dog. _____

19.  We had our own business. _____

20.  He had five dollars in his pocket. _____

**The letter** s **in English is sometimes pronounced like** s **and sometimes like** z.

| /s/ | /z/ |
|-----|-----|
| class | does |
| bus | busy |
| cost | his |
| miss | goes |

*Practice listening to and pronouncing the different* s *sounds. Write* s *or* z *to show how the letter is pronounced.*

1.  also            *s*
2.  busy            *z*
3.  this            _____
4.  these           _____
5.  those           _____
6.  was             _____
7.  class           _____
8.  his             _____
9.  goes            _____
10. some            _____
11. first           _____
12. cousin          _____
13. tries           _____
14. cats            _____
15. movies          _____
16. case            _____
17. kiss            _____
18. plays           _____
19. dogs            _____
20. puts            _____
21. likes           _____
22. brings          _____

23. has             _____
24. closed          _____
25. dress           _____
26. easy            _____
27. pens            _____
28. eyes            _____
29. books           _____
30. nose            _____
31. knows           _____
32. tennis          _____
33. noise           _____
34. bus             _____
35. news            _____
36. house           _____
37. raise           _____
38. peas            _____
39. works           _____
40. days            _____
41. does            _____
42. comes           _____
43. eats            _____
44. rose            _____

### opposites 2

*Write the opposites of the following words.*

| | | | | | | |
|---|---|---|---|---|---|---|
| 1. | night | *day* | | 25. | big | _____ |
| 2. | down | *up* | | 26. | good | _____ |
| 3. | out | _____ | | 27. | safe | _____ |
| 4. | rough | _____ | | 28. | dirty | _____ |
| 5. | dry | _____ | | 29. | dark | _____ |
| 6. | false | _____ | | 30. | late | _____ |
| 7. | last | _____ | | 31. | empty | _____ |
| 8. | before | _____ | | 32. | summer | _____ |
| 9. | husband | _____ | | 33. | fast | _____ |
| 10. | bring | _____ | | 34. | east | _____ |
| 11. | poor | _____ | | 35. | north | _____ |
| 12. | girl | _____ | | 36. | easy | _____ |
| 13. | sister | _____ | | 37. | sit | _____ |
| 14. | soft | _____ | | 38. | sour | _____ |
| 15. | absent | _____ | | 39. | young | _____ |
| 16. | woman | _____ | | 40. | present | _____ |
| 17. | wet | _____ | | 41. | dull | _____ |
| 18. | rude | _____ | | 42. | full | _____ |
| 19. | wife | _____ | | 43. | stand | _____ |
| 20. | daughter | _____ | | 44. | pull | _____ |
| 21. | black | _____ | | 45. | buy | _____ |
| 22. | sharp | _____ | | 46. | near | _____ |
| 23. | married | _____ | | 47. | loose | _____ |
| 24. | sad | _____ | | 48. | inside | _____ |

*Change the words in italics to the correct personal pronouns.*
*Use* I, you, he, she, it, we, they, me, him, her, us, *or* them.

1.  *The book* is on the desk.                              *It*
2.  *Mr. Cortez* is in his office.                          _____
3.  *John and his brother* are in the cafeteria.            _____
4.  I saw *Pamela* yesterday.                               _____
5.  Do you study with *George?*                             _____
6.  Yes, I study with *George and his sister.*              _____
7.  *This book* is new.                                     _____
8.  *Those books* are old.                                  _____
9.  We see *Annette* on the bus every morning.              _____
10. She has *her lesson* at one o'clock.                    _____
11. I put *your hat and coat* on the chair.                 _____
12. I put *your umbrella* in the corner.                    _____
13. *Alma and I* like to study English.                     _____
14. I saw *you and George* on the bus this morning.         _____
15. *The maid* opened the door for me.                      _____
16. He writes many letters to *his son.*                    _____
17. *The weather* is very cold today.                       _____
18. He put *his hat* on and left the room.                  _____
19. *His son and daughter* live with him.                   _____
20. I know *his son and daughter* very well.                _____
21. He always speaks to *Mary and me* in English.           _____
22. *Mary and I* want to learn English well.                _____
23. *Mike* is a good student.                               _____
24. I like *George* very much.                              _____

*Write the plural form of the following words.*

1. tomato    *tomatoes*
2. dish    _____
3. child    _____
4. city    _____
5. book    _____
6. knife    _____
7. box    _____
8. potato    _____
9. class    _____
10. bus    _____
11. street    _____
12. exercise    _____
13. wish    _____
14. copy    _____
15. pen    _____
16. key    _____
17. church    _____
18. hero    _____
19. woman    _____
20. piano    _____
21. half    _____
22. brother    _____

23. leaf    _____
24. dress    _____
25. sister    _____
26. match    _____
27. letter    _____
28. hat    _____
29. man    _____
30. lunch    _____
31. foot    _____
32. roof    _____
33. echo    _____
34. lady    _____
35. mouse    _____
36. wife    _____
37. boy    _____
38. monkey    _____
39. kiss    _____
40. face    _____
41. dog    _____
42. watch    _____
43. tooth    _____
44. window    _____

**To form the future tense, the auxiliary** will **is used with the simple form of the verb. The contracted form (**'ll**) is generally used.**

| | |
|---|---|
| I will run. (I'll run.) | We will run. (We'll run.) |
| You will run. (You'll run.) | You will run. (You'll run.) |
| He will run. (He'll run.) | They will run. (They'll run.) |
| She will run. (She'll run.) | |
| It will run. (It'll run.) | |

*Change to the future tense. Write the complete verb in the blanks.*

1. He studies in this class.                    *will study*
2. She works in this office.                    _____
3. You speak English well.                      _____
4. I come to the lesson on time.                _____
5. They walk to their work.                     _____
6. He brings his friends to class.              _____
7. He opens the door for us.                     _____
8. He studies at the library.                    _____
9. She brings all her books to the lesson.       _____
10. She plays the violin well.                    _____
11. We carry all the small packages.              _____
12. She speaks to us in English.                  _____
13. He writes a letter to his mother every day.   _____
14. I bring you many presents.                    _____
15. She arrives at the studio on time.            _____
16. He has his lesson in this room.               _____
17. They eat all their meals in the cafeteria.    _____
18. The train leaves at eight o'clock.            _____
19. You like that teacher very much.              _____
20. She teaches us English and mathematics.       _____

**The future tense of** to be **is** will be. **The contracted form** ('ll) **is generally used.**

| | |
|---|---|
| I will be (I'll be) | we will be (we'll be) |
| you will be (you'll be) | you will be (you'll be) |
| he will be (he'll be) | they will be (they'll be) |
| she will be (she'll be) | |
| it will be (it'll be) | |

There will be **is contracted** there'll be.

*Change to the future tense. Use only the contracted forms.*

1.  He is in the cafeteria.      *He'll be* 
2.  They are on the second floor. _____
3.  She is your new teacher. _____
4.  He is a good swimmer. _____
5.  It is on the desk. _____
6.  I am in the second class. _____
7.  You are in Chicago. _____
8.  He is a big boy. _____
9.  It is your room. _____
10. We are very busy. _____
11. You are the youngest winner of the prize. _____
12. There is a table in the room. _____
13. She is very tired after each tournament. _____
14. They are at home. _____
15. It is very warm during this season of the year. _____
16. He is out of town all week. _____
17. I am glad to know her. _____
18. She is a very intelligent child. _____
19. We are in the first class. _____
20. They are easy for her to make. _____

## 55 Future tense:

### negative form with *will*

**Form the negative of the future tense by placing** not **after the auxiliary** will. **Notice how the contracted form in the negative is** won't **in all three persons, both singular and plural.**

| | | |
|---|---|---|
| I will not move. | (I won't move.) | We will not move. |
| You will not move. | (You won't move.) | (We won't move.) |
| He will not move. | (He won't move.) | You will not move. |
| She will not move. | (She won't move.) | (You won't move.) |
| It will not move. | (It won't move.) | They will not move. |
| | | (They won't move.) |

*Change to the negative form. Use only the contracted forms.*

1.  He will see us at three o'clock.      *won't see*
2.  She will be back in an hour. _____
3.  He will be the best student in the class. _____
4.  They will arrive on the two o'clock train. _____
5.  She will meet us here. _____
6.  I will bring the medicine with me. _____
7.  He will wait for us on the corner. _____
8.  They will return next month. _____
9.  She will help us with the work. _____
10. I will leave at three o'clock. _____
11. She will sign her name to the letter. _____
12. He will eat with us. _____
13. I will be able to meet you. _____
14. I will see you next Wednesday. _____
15. She will write to you again. _____
16. He will be in Washington next week. _____
17. We will tell Sally about it. _____
18. He will be interested in the news. _____
19. You will like that picture very much. _____
20. The weather will be warm tomorrow. _____

### question form with *will*

**Form yes-no questions in the future tense by placing** will **before the subject. The same order is used even with question-word questions.**

| | |
|---|---|
| will I go | will we go |
| will you go | will you go |
| will he go | will they go |
| will she go | |
| will it go | |
| What time will you arrive? | How many will she buy? |
| When will I see you again? | Who will they visit? |

**In statements with** there will be, there **is treated like a subject.**

| | |
|---|---|
| There will be a party next week. | Will there be a party next week? |

*Change to the question form. Write the complete verb and subject in the blanks.*

1. He will return next week.      *Will he return*
2. She will write a novel. _____
3. They will leave for California on Wednesday. _____
4. He will be out of town all month. _____
5. He will study at the University of Miami. _____
6. We will have our lesson at two o'clock. _____
7. He will pay $2,000 for the car. _____
8. They will make good progress. _____
9. Rita will be here in an hour. _____
10. We will write her a letter immediately. _____
11. They will wait for us on the corner. _____
12. The lesson will begin at ten o'clock. _____
13. The movie will end at 7 pm. _____
14. The meeting will last for more than an hour. _____
15. She will speak English well someday. _____
16. They will turn out to be good friends. _____
17. They will travel to both France and England during the summer. _____
18. There will be many students absent tomorrow. _____
19. You will have many exercises to prepare for tomorrow. _____

## *to be,* present, past, future

*Write the correct tense of* to be *in the blanks.*

1. a. John _____ in the cafeteria *now.*          *is*
   b. John _____ in the cafeteria *yesterday.*     *was*
   c. John _____ in the cafeteria *tomorrow.*      *will be*

2. a. They _____ in Mr. Smith's office *now.*          _____
   b. They _____ in Mr. Smith's office *yesterday.*    _____
   c. They _____ in Mr. Smith's office *tomorrow.*     _____

3. a. She _____ sick *today.*       _____
   b. She _____ sick *yesterday.*   _____
   c. She _____ sick *tomorrow.*    _____

4. a. We _____ very busy *today.*       _____
   b. We _____ very busy *yesterday.*   _____
   c. We _____ very busy *tomorrow.*    _____

5. a. Helen and Marc _____ in this class *now.*          _____
   b. Helen and Marc _____ in this class *yesterday.*    _____
   c. Helen and Marc _____ in this class *tomorrow.*     _____

6. a. There _____ many students absent *today.*       _____
   b. There _____ many students absent *yesterday.*   _____
   c. There _____ many students absent *tomorrow.*    _____

7. a. Mr. Rubio _____ out of town *today.*       _____
   b. Mr. Rubio _____ out of town *yesterday.*   _____
   c. Mr. Rubio _____ out of town *tomorrow.*    _____

8. a. These exercises _____ easy for me *now.*          _____
   b. These exercises _____ easy for me *yesterday.*    _____
   c. These exercises _____ easy for me *tomorrow.*     _____

9. a. I _____ very tired *today.*       _____
   b. I _____ very tired *yesterday.*   _____
   c. I _____ very tired *tomorrow.*    _____

### negative form

*Change to the negative form. Use contractions. In the future tense, be sure to write the auxiliary and the main verb in your answer.*

1.  a.  He is in the cafeteria *now.*                                    *isn't*
    b.  He was in the cafeteria *yesterday.*                             *wasn't*
    c.  He will be in the cafeteria *tomorrow.*                          *won't be*

2.  a.  Mr. and Mrs. Reese are out of town *today.*                      _____
    b.  Mr. and Mrs. Reese were out of town *yesterday.*                 _____
    c.  Mr. and Mrs. Reese will be out of town *tomorrow.*              _____

3.  a.  You are very busy *today.*                                        _____
    b.  You were very busy *yesterday.*                                   _____
    c.  You will be very busy *tomorrow.*                                 _____

4.  a.  There are many students absent from class *today.*                _____
    b.  There were many students absent from class
        *yesterday.*                                                     _____
    c.  There will be many students absent from class
        *tomorrow.*                                                      _____

5.  a.  The weather is very good *today.*                                 _____
    b.  The weather was very good *yesterday.*                            _____
    c.  The weather will be very good *tomorrow.*                         _____

6.  a.  The doors are closed *now.*                                       _____
    b.  The doors were closed *yesterday.*                                _____
    c.  The doors will be closed *tomorrow.*                              _____

7.  a.  Lee and I are in the same class *now.*                            _____
    b.  Lee and I were in the same class *last year.*                     _____
    c.  Lee and I will be in the same class *next year.*                  _____

8.  a.  The lesson *today* is easy.                                       _____
    b.  The lesson *yesterday* was easy.                                  _____
    c.  The lesson *tomorrow* will be easy.                               _____

## 59 Review: *to be*, present, past, future, question form

*Change to the question form. Write the complete verb and subject in the blanks.*

1. a. They are in Ellen's office *now.*      *Are they*
   b. They were in Ellen's office *yesterday.*      *Were they*
   c. They will be in Ellen's office *tomorrow.*      *Will they be*

2. a. The door is open *now.*      _____
   b. The door was open *yesterday.*      _____
   c. The door will be open *tomorrow.*      _____

3. a. It is very cold *today.*      _____
   b. It was very cold *yesterday.*      _____
   c. It will be very cold *tomorrow.*      _____

4. a. They are in Europe *now.*      _____
   b. They were in Europe *last summer.*      _____
   c. They will be in Europe *next summer.*      _____

5. a. There are many new words in *today's* lesson.      _____
   b. There were many new words in *yesterday's* lesson.      _____
   c. There will be many new words in *tomorrow's* lesson.      _____

6. a. Felipe is in my English class *now.*      _____
   b. Felipe was in my English class *last year.*      _____
   c. Felipe will be in my English class *next year.*      _____

7. a. The exercises are very hard *today.*      _____
   b. The exercises were very hard *yesterday.*      _____
   c. The exercises will be very hard *tomorrow.*      _____

8. a. We are tired after our walk in the park *today.*      _____
   b. We were tired after our walk in the park *yesterday.*      _____
   c. We will be tired after our walk in the park *tomorrow.*      _____

9. a. The train is late *today.*      _____
   b. The train was late *yesterday.*      _____
   c. The train will be late *tomorrow.*      _____

### and future tenses

*Write the correct form of the verb in the blanks.*

1.  a.  He (come) to school by bus *every day.*       *comes*
    b.  He _____ to school by bus *yesterday.*       *came*
    c.  He _____ to school by bus *tomorrow.*       *will come*

2.  a.  They (eat) in the cafeteria *every day.*       _____
    b.  They _____ in the cafeteria *yesterday.*       _____
    c.  They _____ in the cafeteria *tomorrow.*       _____

3.  a.  I (have) lunch with him *every day.*       _____
    b.  I _____ lunch with him *yesterday.*       _____
    c.  I _____ lunch with him *tomorrow.*       _____

4.  a.  We (arrive) on time for the lesson *every day.*       _____
    b.  We _____ on time for the lesson *yesterday.*       _____
    c.  We _____ on time for the lesson *tomorrow.*       _____

5.  a.  Ms. Bao (take) her car to work *every day.*       _____
    b.  Ms. Bao _____ her car to work *yesterday.*       _____
    c.  Ms. Bao _____ her car to work *tomorrow.*       _____

6.  a.  Helen (go) to the movies *every night.*       _____
    b.  Helen _____ to the movies *last night.*       _____
    c.  Helen _____ to the movies *tomorrow night.*       _____

7.  a.  He (wait) for me on the corner *every day.*       _____
    b.  He _____ for me on the corner *yesterday.*       _____
    c.  He _____ for me on the corner *tomorrow.*       _____

8.  a.  Our lesson (end) at three o'clock *every day.*       _____
    b.  Our lesson _____ at three o'clock *yesterday.*       _____
    c.  Our lesson _____ at three o'clock *tomorrow.*       _____

9.  a.  Mary and Linda (get) up early *every morning.*       _____
    b.  Mary and Linda _____ up early *yesterday morning.*       _____
    c.  Mary and Linda _____ up early *tomorrow morning.*       _____

### negative form

*Change to the negative form. Use* do, does, did, *or* will *in the contracted form, and include the main verb in your answer.*

1. a. She studies in our group.                                    *doesn't study*
   b. She studied in our group last year.                   *didn't study*
   c. She will study in our group next year.          *won't study*

2. a. They live in Mexico now.                                  _____
   b. They lived in Mexico last year.                         _____
   c. They will live in Mexico next year.                   _____

3. a. She comes here every afternoon.                     _____
   b. She came here yesterday afternoon.               _____
   c. She will come here tomorrow afternoon.        _____

4. a. I have my lunch at twelve o'clock every day.   _____
   b. I had my lunch at twelve o'clock yesterday.    _____
   c. I will have my lunch at twelve o'clock tomorrow.   _____

5. a. We go to the movies every Wednesday night.   _____
   b. We went to the movies last Wednesday night.   _____
   c. We will go to the movies next Wednesday night.   _____

6. a. Our lesson begins at two o'clock.                    _____
   b. Our lesson began at two o'clock yesterday.      _____
   c. Our lesson will begin at two o'clock tomorrow.   _____

7. a. Paul and Mary read the newspaper every morning.   _____
   b. Paul and Mary read the newspaper yesterday morning._____
   c. Paul and Mary will read the newspaper tomorrow
      morning.                                                              _____

8. a. You get up early every morning.                       _____
   b. You got up early yesterday morning.                 _____
   c. You will get up early tomorrow morning.         _____

## question form

*Change to the question form. Use* do, does, did, *or will before the subject, and include the main verb in your answer.*

1. a. She comes to school by bus every day.     *Does she come*
   b. She came to school by bus yesterday.     *Did she come*
   c. She will come to school by bus tomorrow.     *Will she come*

2. a. The train leaves at two o'clock every afternoon.     _____
   b. The train left at two o'clock yesterday afternoon.     _____
   c. The train will leave at two o'clock tomorrow afternoon.     _____

3. a. Our lesson ends at one o'clock.     _____
   b. Our lesson ended at one o'clock yesterday.     _____
   c. Our lesson will end at one o'clock tomorrow.     _____

4. a. We eat dinner at home every night.     _____
   b. We ate dinner at home last night.     _____
   c. We will eat dinner at home tomorrow night.     _____

5. a. The bus stops at this corner.     _____
   b. The bus stopped at this corner.     _____
   c. The bus will stop at this corner.     _____

6. a. Peter gets up at seven o'clock every morning.     _____
   b. Peter got up at seven o'clock yesterday morning.     _____
   c. Peter will get up at seven o'clock tomorrow morning.     _____

7. a. She writes to her parents every day.     _____
   b. She wrote to her parents yesterday.     _____
   c. She will write to her parents tomorrow.     _____

8. a. John goes to bed early every night.     _____
   b. John went to bed early last night.     _____
   c. John will go to bed early tomorrow night.     _____

9. a. They wake up early every morning.     _____
   b. They woke up early this morning.     _____
   c. They will wake up early tomorrow morning.     _____

**Adjectives modify nouns.**

a beautiful day      an interesting idea

**Adverbs modify verbs by telling us how we do something.**

She works quietly.   They write clearly.

**Many adverbs are formed by adding** ly **to the adjective.**

easy-easily   careful-carefully   nice-nicely

**A few words, like** fast, hard, late, **and** low, **take the same form as both adjectives and adverbs.**

It was a late movie.     I stayed out late.
She had a hard time.   She studied hard.

*Write the correct form, adjective or adverb, in the blanks.*

1. She is a (beautiful) girl.  *beautiful*
2. Lisa plays the piano (beautiful).  *beautifully*
3. This apple is (soft).  _____
4. Miss Levine always speaks very (soft).  _____
5. Albert did the work very (clever).  _____
6. He is very (clever) boy.  _____
7. Frances always prepares her lessons (careful).  _____
8. She is also a (careful) cook.  _____
9. Martin walked (slow) because he was tired.  _____
10. I was late because my watch was (slow).  _____
11. She dressed (quick) to save time.  _____
12. It was a (quick) lunch because they wanted to go shopping.  _____
13. It isn't (easy) to lose weight.  _____
14. Martha won the race (easy).  _____
15. I see him at work (frequent).  _____
16. He is a (frequent) visitor to my office.  _____
17. Alice and Rose are (serious) students of Russian.  _____

Good *is an adjective. It always modifies a noun.*

> They are *good* pictures.

Well *is usually used as an adverb.*

> They work *well* by themselves.

Well *can be used as an adjective when it means "to be in good health."*

> He was sick, but now he's well.

*Write* good *or* well *in the blanks.*

1. Tony is a very _____ student.                                        *good*
2. She always prepares her lessons _____.                               *well*
3. Carlos speaks English _____.                                         _____
4. Our lesson today was very _____.                                     _____
5. The movie last night was very _____.                                 _____
6. Alice plays chess _____.                                             _____
7. Brian always does his work _____.                                    _____
8. Clara plays the piano _____.                                         _____
9. She is also a _____ tennis player.                                   _____
10. We will soon speak English _____.                                   _____
11. I don't think she sings _____.                                      _____
12. My new car runs _____.                                              _____
13. It seems to be a very _____ pen.                                    _____
14. I was sick for several weeks, but I am _____ now.                   _____
15. Luiz can swim _____.                                                _____
16. His brother is also a _____ swimmer.                                _____
17. Emma dances very _____.                                             _____
18. Helen is also a very _____ dancer.                                  _____
19. Everything William does he does _____.                             _____
20. Mr. Rice, our English teacher, also speaks French very _____.       _____
21. But is he a _____ English teacher?                                  _____

**Much** *is used with uncountable nouns. These are nouns which cannot be counted and which do not have a plural form.*

much sugar   much rain   much money   much time

**Many** *is used with countable nouns in the plural.*

many cups of sugar   many people   many dollars   many hours

*A lot of* **is used for both** much **and** many. A lot of **is used more frequently than either** much **or** many.

a lot of sugar   a lot of rain   a lot of money   a lot of books

*Use* much *or* many *with the following words or phrases.*

| | | | | | |
|---|---|---|---|---|---|
| 1. | *many* | windows | 23. | _____ | coffee |
| 2. | *much* | smoke | 24. | _____ | tea |
| 3. | _____ | apples | 25. | _____ | cups of tea |
| 4. | _____ | pace | 26. | _____ | trouble |
| 5. | _____ | people | 27. | _____ | effort |
| 6. | _____ | birds | 28. | _____ | plants |
| 7. | _____ | fruit | 29. | _____ | flowers |
| 8. | _____ | sugar | 30. | _____ | strength |
| 9. | _____ | rooms | 31. | _____ | homework |
| 10. | _____ | work | 32. | _____ | friends |
| 11. | _____ | students | 33. | _____ | conversation |
| 12. | _____ | windows | 34. | _____ | news |
| 13. | _____ | butter | 35. | _____ | seats |
| 14. | _____ | meat | 36. | _____ | mistakes |
| 15. | _____ | exercises | 37. | _____ | vegetables |
| 16. | _____ | time | 38. | _____ | bread |
| 17. | _____ | times | 39. | _____ | letters |
| 18. | _____ | snow | 40. | _____ | salt |
| 19. | _____ | money | 41. | _____ | pepper |
| 20. | _____ | rain | 42. | _____ | mustard |
| 21. | _____ | cups of coffee | 43. | _____ | pens |
| 22. | _____ | wind | 44. | _____ | ink |

## 66   No, not

No **is an adjective.**

> They have *no* friends in the city.

Not **is generally used as an adverb to make a sentence negative.**

> He does *not* speak much English.
> I did *not* finish on time.

Not **can also be used before a noun modified by an article or a numeral.**

> *Not* a day passed without rain.   *Not* one person spoke.

*Write* no *or* not *in the blanks.*

1.  That room has _____ windows in it.       *no*
2.  He does _____ attend class regularly.  _____
3.  There are _____ boys in our English class.  _____
4.  Today is _____ Friday.  _____
5.  There was _____ much money in her purse.  _____
6.  _____ one girl wanted to dance with him.  _____
7.  We have _____ time to talk about that now.  _____
8.  _____ person wants that job.  _____
9.  There are _____ many students in the cafeteria now.  _____
10.  Teresa has _____ English book.  _____
11.  Does Peter spend much time on his English?
    No, _____ much!  _____
12.  I have _____ time to study.  _____
13.  There are _____ many students absent today.  _____
14.  In fact, there are _____ students absent at all.  _____
15.  He has _____ money to spend on books.  _____
16.  She is _____ a good student.  _____
17.  There is _____ a really serious student in the
    whole class.  _____
18.  This exercise is _____ difficult.  _____

# 67 Irregular verbs:

## past tense 3

*Study and memorize the past tense forms of the following irregular verbs.*

| become | became | find | found | shake | shook |
|--------|--------|------|-------|-------|-------|
| bring | brought | forget | forgot | sing | sang |
| break | broke | lose | lost | take | took |
| catch | caught | make | made | teach | taught |
| fight | fought | ring | rang | think | thought |

*Change the following sentences to the past tense.*

1. She sings very well.     *sang*
2. It takes two weeks to go there by train. _____
3. She brings her brother to class. _____
4. I forget his name. _____
5. Ms. Sung teaches us both English and mathematics. _____
6. She loses a lot of money in the lottery. _____
7. The bell rings at three o'clock every day. _____
8. The weather becomes very warm in the desert. _____
9. She makes many mistakes in spelling. _____
10. The teacher finds many mistakes in our compositions. _____
11. The boxers shake hands before the fight. _____
12. I catch cold very easily. _____
13. He fights with his brother continually. _____
14. He thinks about his troubles all the time. _____
15. She becomes very tired of the same routine. _____
16. They take three English lessons each week. _____
17. The cat catches many mice. _____
18. Robert forgets to bring his books to class. _____
19. Our telephone rings during the day. _____
20. Mr. Matos makes a good salary in his job. _____
21. I break too many dishes. _____
22. Olga and her sister both sing very well. _____

*Write the correct prepositions in the blanks.*

1.  She gave the money _____ her son.                          *to*
2.  The plane fell _____ the river.                            _____
3.  She went to the store _____ some bread.                    _____
4.  The animal jumped _____ a hole in the ground.              _____
5.  When did he leave _____ New York?                          _____
6.  Did he go _____ plane?                                     _____
7.  She wants to hang the picture _____ the fireplace.         _____
8.  You can put your coat _____ that chair.                    _____
9.  The airplane flew _____ the city.                          _____
10. Hurry or you will be late _____ the lesson.                _____
11. Don't wait _____ him any longer.                           _____
12. He will return _____ his native country.                   _____
13. Then he will return _____ his native country.              _____
14. We must study from page 10 _____ page 12
    for tomorrow's lesson.                                       _____
15. He took a handkerchief _____ his pocket.                   _____
16. We walked _____ the river for about an hour.               _____
17. The teacher sits _____ front of the class.                 _____
18. For the class picture, the tall students stood
    _____ the short ones.                                      _____
19. Is Philadelphia _____ Pittsburgh or far from it?           _____
20. Ms. Rossi asked me all _____ my trip to Las Vegas.         _____
21. The bus doesn't stop _____ this corner.                    _____
22. Did he leave a message _____ me?                           _____
23. I must look _____ the pencil which I lost.                 _____
24. Penny looked _____ me and smiled.                          _____

## 69 Vocabulary review:

### mistakes of fact 2

*The items in boldface are mistakes. Change them to make the facts correct, and write your answers in the blanks.*

1. The last month of the year is **January**.    *December*
2. The capital of the United States is **New York City**.    _____
3. The largest state in the United States is **California**.    _____
4. The smallest state in the United States is **Connecticut**.    _____
5. Ten plus four is **thirteen**.    _____
6. Ten minus four is **seven**.    _____
7. Ten times four is **thirty-five**.    _____
8. Winter begins officially on **November** 21.    _____
9. Summer begin officially on **July** 21.    _____
10. February comes **after** March.    _____
11. August comes **before** July.    _____
12. The opposite of *expensive* is **new**.    _____
13. The opposite of *east* is **north**.    _____
14. There are **fifty** seconds in a minute.    _____
15. The past tense of *see* is **said**.    _____
16. The past tense of *sit* is **set**.    _____
17. The plural form of *this* is **those**.    _____
18. The auxiliary verb for the future tense is **did**.    _____
19. People hear with their **eyes**.    _____
20. Lemons are generally **sweet**.    _____
21. Before we go out, we usually **take off** our hats and coats.    _____
22. *Right away* means **later**.    _____
23. If I am *thirsty*, I want something to **eat**.    _____
24. We pronounce the word *walked* as a word of **two syllables**.    _____

*Select the correct answer and write it in the space provided.*

1.  The opposite of *black* is (blue, yellow, green, white).          *white*

2.  The last month of the year is
    (November, December, October, July).          _____

3.  The next to the last month of the year is
    (October, December, November, July).          _____

4.  Which of the following is a fruit: horse, radio, pair, pear?          _____

5.  Which letter in the word *wrist* is silent (not pronounced)?          _____

6.  Which letter in the word *knife* is silent (not pronounced)?          _____

7.  Which of these past tense forms do we pronounce
    as a word of one syllable: counted, asked, pointed, waited?          _____

8.  We pronounce the contraction *I'll* to rhyme with
    (will, mile, shall, girl).          _____

9.  We pronounce the contraction *she's* to rhyme with
    (this, those, sneeze, miss).          _____

10. We pronounce the word *thumb* to rhyme with
    (room, soon, some, then).          _____

11. The word *newspaper* has three syllables. On which syllable
    do we accent the word—the first, second, or third syllable?          _____

12. The opposite of *lose* is (place, find, take, bring).          _____

13. We pronounce the word *crossed* to rhyme with
    (lose, loose, east, lost).          _____

14. *Lately* means (sometimes, very soon, much later, recently).          _____

15. The past tense form of *can* is (may, could, might, should).          _____

16. Which of these do we use in a restaurant:
    blackboard, chalk, menu, eraser?          _____

17. Which of these do we use when it rains: pencil,
    umbrella, fork, sweater?          _____

*Select the correct form. Write your answers in the blanks.*

1. This car (belong, belongs) to Mr. Lewis.            *belongs*
2. Yesterday Mr. Lewis (come, came) to school by bus.  _____
3. What time (do, did) you get up this morning?        _____
4. Mr. Molavi is (a, an) Iranian.                      _____
5. Sally and I (was, were) both sick yesterday.        _____
6. He spends (a lot of, many) time on his English.     _____
7. Angela (can speak, can to speak) French well.       _____
8. Paul (have, has) many friends in this school.       _____
9. Peter teaches (we, us) English and mathematics.     _____
10. (Do, Does) Mr. Dulac speak Spanish well?           _____
11. (No, Not) one person in our class went to the party. _____
12. (No, Not) many people attended the meeting.        _____
13. Tracy (catch, caught) cold at the beach yesterday. _____
14. Martha plays the piano (good, well).               _____
15. She also sings (beautiful, beautifully).           _____
16. Roger always prepares his lesson (careful, carefully). _____
17. (Tomatos, Tomatoes) are my favorite vegetable.     _____
18. The (leafs, leaves) fall from the trees in October. _____
19. We saw (they, them) on the bus yesterday.          _____
20. I spoke to him (by, on) the telephone yesterday.   _____
21. (Was, Were) Leslie absent from class yesterday?    _____
22. (Do, Does) Mark live near you?                     _____
23. (Do, Does) you live near Sam?                      _____
24. (Do, Does) Colette and you have much homework
    for tomorrow?                                      _____
25. Susana is (a, an) old friend.                      _____

**To form the present continuous tense, place the correct form of** to be **before the present participle form (the** ing **form) of the main verb. The contraction is normally used.**

| | |
|---|---|
| I am going (I'm going) | we are going (we're going) |
| you are going (you're going) | you are going (you're going) |
| he is going (he's going) | they are going (they're going) |
| she is going (she's going) | |
| it is going (it's going) | |

**The present continuous tense describes an action which is happening at the present moment.**

She's working on the problem now.   They're leaving now.

*Complete the sentences with the present continuous tense of the verb in parentheses.*

1.  Martin (do) his homework now.                                *is doing*
2.  She (wait) for me on the corner now.                 _____
3.  Look! It (begin) to rain.                                        _____
4.  The leaves (begin) to fall from the trees.          _____
5.  They (take) a walk along Fifth Avenue.             _____
6.  I (begin) to understand English grammar now.  _____
7.  We (make) good progress in our courses.          _____
8.  Listen! The telephone (ring).                             _____
9.  We (study) the exercise now.                             _____
10. The train (leave) at this moment.                      _____
11. Elizabeth (look) for her English book.               _____
12. Listen! Someone (knock) at the door.                _____
13. Look! Mr. Salas (walk) in our direction.            _____
14. My father (read) the newspaper now.                _____
15. The wind (blow) very hard now.                        _____
16. The teacher (look) directly at you.                    _____
17. All the students (laugh) at you.                         _____
18. The bus (stop) for us now.                                _____
19. Mr. and Mrs. Nomura (build) a new home on First Street. _____

**The present continuous tense describes what is happening now. The simple present tense describes what happens all the time or every day. Note the differences of the meanings below.**

> Erica is talking to Jan now. (present continuous)
> Erica talks to Jan every day. (simple present)

*Complete the sentences with the present continuous tense or the simple present tense of the verb in parentheses.*

1.  Our telephone (ring) often.                                       *rings*
2.  The telephone (ring) now                                          *is ringing*
3.  Ana always (do) her lessons well.                                 _____
4.  Look! It (begin) to snow.                                         _____
5.  The wind (blow) the leaves across the field.                      _____
6.  Ms. Adams (smoke) too much.                                       _____
7.  Look! She (smoke) a cigarette now.                                _____
8.  Mimi (write) to her brother once a week.                          _____
9.  She (write) a letter to her brother now.                          _____
10. Look! Janet (wave) to us from the other side of the street. _____
11. Listen! Someone (walk) around downstairs.                         _____
12. We always (have) a good time at Helen's parties.                  _____
13. Claude (have) his breakfast now.                                  _____
14. We (have) English lessons three times a week.                     _____
15. We (have) our English class now.                                  _____
16. The bus always (stop) at this corner.                             _____
17. The bus (stop) for us now.                                        _____
18. Look! Alex (get) off the bus now.                                 _____
19. He always (get) off the bus at this corner.                       _____
20. Mr. and Mrs. Eng (buy) a new home on Second Street.               _____

*Change the simple present tense to the present continuous tense. Be sure you understand the change in meaning which occurs with these verb changes.*

1. Henri *studies* in this class.    *is studying*
2. She *goes* to the movies.    _____
3. They *come* to visit us.    _____
4. The wind *blows* very hard.    _____
5. The leaves *fall* from the trees.    _____
6. The teacher *corrects* our compositions.    _____
7. Alice *prepares* her homework carefully.    _____
8. The bus *stops* at this corner.    _____
9. He *drives* to work in his car.    _____
10. The train *leaves* on time.    _____
11. He *helps* Marie with her homework.    _____
12. He *eats* lunch in the cafeteria.    _____
13. She *does* her work well.    _____
14. He *wears* a dark suit.    _____
15. She *waits* for me on this corner.    _____
16. We *learn* English rapidly.    _____
17. She *prepares* dinner for the whole family.    _____
18. She *wears* running shoes.    _____
19. Martha *plays* the piano.    _____
20. He *speaks* very slowly.    _____
21. She *teaches* us English.    _____
22. He *puts* cream in his coffee.    _____

## negative form

**Form the negative of the present continuous tense by placing** not **after the auxiliary** to be. **The contracted forms are generally used.**

> She is using the word processor.
> She *is not using (isn't using)* the word processor.

*Change the following sentences from the affirmative to the negative form. Use the contracted forms.*

1. He is doing his homework now.                                *isn't doing*
2. The telephone is ringing.                                   _____
3. The leaves are changing color.                              _____
4. We are making good progress.                                _____
5. I am learning many new words.                               _____
6. They are selling a new home on Second Street.               _____
7. The bus is stopping for us.                                 _____
8. I am having a good time.                                    _____
9. She is having her lunch now.                                _____
10. He is reading the newspaper now.                           _____
11. They are watching television now.                          _____
12. She is doing well in her new job.                          _____
13. They are traveling in South America now.                   _____
14. He is laughing at you.                                     _____
15. The teacher is looking at us.                              _____
16. They are speaking English.                                 _____
17. The wind is blowing hard.                                  _____
18. The sky is getting dark.                                   _____
19. I am getting hungry.                                       _____
20. The weather is turning cold.                               _____
21. The clerk is showing us the VCR.                           _____
22. She is taking medicine for her cold.                       _____

## question form

**To form questions in the present continuous tense, place the auxiliary** to be **before the subject.**

| | |
|---|---|
| I am taking computer classes. | Am I taking computer classes? |
| She is studying photography. | Is she studying photography? |

*Change to the question form. Write the complete verb and subject in the blanks.*

1. He is doing his homework now.      *Is he doing*
2. She is waiting for us on the corner.    _____
3. The telephone is ringing in the other room.   _____
4. The police are investigating the accident now.   _____
5. The mail carrier is delivering the mail now.   _____
6. The birds are flying south for the winter.   _____
7. They are taking a walk in the park.   _____
8. Adam is reading the newspaper.   _____
9. Roy is preparing dinner for the whole family.   _____
10. They are taking computer classes.   _____
11. The sky is getting very dark.   _____
12. The wind is beginning to blow very hard.   _____
13. William is becoming an expert in English grammar.   _____
14. Her cousin is studying to be a doctor.   _____
15. They are discussing the examinations.   _____
16. Sara's family is moving to Chicago.   _____
17. The bus is stopping for us now.   _____
18. She is getting very hungry.   _____
19. He is signing the letters now.   _____
20. They are shaking hands like old friends.   _____
21. Annette is being particularly friendly with him.   _____
22. Mr. Berger is taking his daughter with him on his trip.   _____

*A common way to form the future tense is to use the appropriate form of* to be going to *and the simple form of the verb. The contracted forms are generally used.*

| | |
|---|---|
| I am (I'm) going to finish soon. | We are (We're) going to finish soon. |
| You are (you're) going to finish soon. | You are (You're) going to finish soon. |
| He is (He's) going to finish soon. | |
| She is (She's) going to finish soon. | They are (They're) going to finish soon. |
| It is (It's) going to finish soon. | |

*Use the appropriate form of* going to *followed by the simple verb to complete the following sentences. Use both the full form and the contracted form.*

1. We (study) English literature next year.   *are going to study*
   *we're going to study*

2. He (meet) us at eight o'clock.   _____
   _____

3. She (buy) a new dress for the dance.   _____
   _____

4. We (go) to Mexico on our vacation.   _____
   _____

5. They (build) a new home on   _____
   Front Street   _____

6. He (take) Grace to the dance tonight.   _____
   _____

7. We (have) a picnic next Saturday.   _____
   _____

8. The paper says that it (rain) tomorrow.   _____
   _____

9. I (have) lunch with Helen today.   _____
   _____

10. She (meet) me outside the cafeteria.   _____
    _____

11. We (watch) television tonight.   _____
    _____

12. He (study) engineering at college.   _____
    _____

13. Julia says that she (be) a doctor when   _____
    she grows up.   _____

**Short answers are usually used to answer direct questions. A short answer consists of the subject of the sentence and an auxiliary verb. Sometimes the auxiliary is the verb** to be.

| | |
|---|---|
| Can you use a computer? | Yes, I can. No, I can't. |
| Are they driving to Canada? | Yes, they are. No, they aren't. |

**Note that we use the contracted form in the negative short answer. Sometimes the auxiliary is the verb** to do.

| | |
|---|---|
| Does she speak Italian? | Yes, she does. No, she doesn't. |
| Do you have a camera? | Yes, I do. No, I don't. |

**When the direct question has a noun, a pronoun is normally used in the short answer.**

| | |
|---|---|
| Does Erica live here? | Yes, she does. No, she doesn't. |
| Will Jan and Fred stay here? | Yes, they will. No, they won't. |

*Answer the questions with short affirmative and negative answers. Use pronouns and contractions where appropriate. Answer* you *questions with* I; *answer* you *and* X *questions with* we.

1. Does Julia live near you?  *Yes, she does.*  *No, she doesn't.*
2. Will you be in class tomorrow?  _____  _____
3. Will Monique be in class tomorrow?  _____  _____
4. Is it raining?  _____  _____
5. Is the telephone ringing?  _____  _____
6. Are there many students in your class?  _____  _____
7. Did you and Eric go to the movies last night?  _____  _____
8. Do you like to study English?  _____  _____
9. Are you going to the movies tonight?  _____  _____
10. Is Tony sick today?  _____  _____
11. Are both windows open?  _____  _____
12. Is this Ms. Duval's office?  _____  _____
13. Are we going to be late for class?  _____  _____
14. Can you meet me after the lesson?  _____  _____
15. Did it rain hard last night?  _____  _____

A **and** an **are indefinite articles. They refer to objects which are not specific.**

> *A* book is on the shelf.

The **is a definite article. It refers to a particular object.**

> *The* book that you gave me is very interesting.

**No article is used when we talk about a general idea or a whole class of objects.**

> *Air* is necessary for life.    *Gold* makes nice jewelry.

**No articles are used with proper nouns, names of persons, cities, streets, or countries. (Exceptions: the United States, the Soviet Union, and the United Kingdom)**

> Frank lives on Connecticut Avenue.    We visited France last summer.

**When a proper noun is used as an adjective, the definite article is used.**

> The Main Street shops are closed on Sunday.

*Write the article, if necessary, in the blanks. If no article is necessary, leave a blank.*

1. _____ water in this glass is dirty.                      *the*
2. Everyone should drink several glasses of _____ water every day.                                              _____
3. _____ water in many cities is not good.          _____
4. _____ New York City has humid weather.       _____
5. _____ climate of Arizona is very dry.             _____
6. Steve is from _____ California.                        _____
7. _____ Michigan shoreline is very long.           _____
8. Elaine lives on _____ Seventh Avenue.           _____
9. I always take _____ Seventh Avenue subway to my work.                                                        _____
10. _____ English is more difficult to learn than French.                                                       _____
11. _____ English language is difficult to learn.  _____
12. We need _____ good light in order to study.   _____
13. _____ light in this classroom is not good.      _____

*Study and memorize the past tense forms of the following irregular verbs.*

| blow | blew | hit | hit | shut | shut |
|------|------|-----|-----|------|------|
| cut | cut | keep | kept | sleep | slept |
| do | did | mean | meant | steal | stole |
| drive | drove | meet | met | sweep | swept |

*Change the following sentences to the past tense.*

1.  I meet her in the cafeteria.                                    *met*
2.  He drives to work in his new car.                        _____
3.  The wind blows hard during the month of March.   _____
4.  We sleep late in the morning.                               _____
5.  The child hits the dog with a stick.                      _____
6.  She sweeps the whole house.                                 _____
7.  Juanita does her homework very carefully.           _____
8.  He steals only from very rich people.                    _____
9.  The word means different things to different people.  _____
10. The cook cuts the meat in the kitchen.                 _____
11. Barbara shuts the windows for the teacher.          _____
12. The fence keeps the children off the lawn.           _____
13. Ms. Sato sleeps only five hours a night.               _____
14. George does me many favors.                               _____
15. They often meet in the park in the afternoon.      _____
16. Ms. Petridis drives her children to school.           _____
17. During a hard storm, the wind blows down some
    of our palm trees.                                              _____
18. This knife cuts very well.                                    _____
19. Children steal the apples from our trees.             _____
20. That light hits me right in the eye.                      _____
21. He keeps all his money in an old box.                  _____

Who *refers to people.* Which *refers to animals or things.*

Which **and** who (whom), **when direct objects of the verb, are often dropped from English sentences. Thus we may say, "Is this the magazine which you want?" or "Is this the magazine you want?" Both forms are correct.**

*Supply* who *or* which *in the following sentences.*

1. His wife, _____ is an accountant, travels often.                    *who*

2. Art books, _____ are very expensive, are in a
   special section.                                                      _____

3. The Statue of Liberty, _____ is in New York Harbor,
   was a gift from France.                                               _____

4. Ms. Rogers, _____ lived in South America for many
   years, speaks Spanish perfectly.                                      _____

5. That pen, _____ my father gave me in 1943,
   is very valuable.                                                     _____

6. The wedding, _____ was held at the bride's home,
   was on June 22.                                                       _____

7. Was it Joe _____ telephoned me?                                    _____

8. The woman _____ is wearing blue is the mother
   of the bride.                                                         _____

9. The bus, _____ is very slow, is the least expensive
   way to go.                                                            _____

10. The students _____ study hard make the best progress.  _____

11. The class, _____ meets only once a week, was canceled.  _____

12. Is this the street on _____ you live?                              _____

13. The movie, _____ got good reviews, is still playing.              _____

14. Our teacher, _____ is a North American, has very
    clear pronunciation.                                                 _____

15. Plant those flowers, _____ need more sun, in back
    of the house.                                                        _____

16. It was Sara _____ left the message for you.                       _____

**The comparative form of a one-syllable adjective adds** er.

| | |
|---|---|
| young-younger | fast-faster |
| smart-smarter | short-shorter |

**The comparative form of adjectives with more than one syllable uses** more.

| | |
|---|---|
| beautiful-more beautiful | interesting-more interesting |
| expensive-more expensive | difficult-more difficult |

**However, two-syllable adjectives that end in** y **or** ow **add** er. **The** y **is changed to** i **before the** er **is added.**

| | |
|---|---|
| heavy-heavier | narrow-narrower |
| sleepy-sleepier | deadly-deadlier |

**The comparative form of adjectives is followed by** than.

| | |
|---|---|
| She's older than her sister. | That's more difficult than you think. |

**The adjectives** good **and** bad **have irregular comparatives:** good-better **and** bad-worse.

| |
|---|
| This movie was better than the other one. |
| The traffic in the city is worse than in the country. |

*Write the comparative form of the adjectives in parentheses. Include the word* than.

1.  Helen is (young) Rob.          *younger than*
2.  This book is (interesting) that one. _____
3.  Oranges are (sweet) lemons. _____
4.  The weather today is (warm) it was yesterday. _____
5.  This exercise is (easy) the last one. _____
6.  Lisa is (intelligent) her sister. _____
7.  The month of February is (cold) the month of March. _____
8.  I am (tired) I was last night. _____
9.  Our classroom is (large) your classroom. _____
10. This lesson is (long) the next one. _____
11. You seem to be (busy) George. _____
12. Her cold is much (bad) mine. _____
13. A dish is (shallow) a bowl. _____

# 83  Adverbs: comparative form

**Adverbs with one syllable take** er **in the comparative form.**

| soon-sooner | late-later |
|---|---|

**Adverbs with more than one syllable take** more **in the comparative form.**

| rapidly-more rapidly | easily-more easily |
|---|---|

**The comparative form of adverbs is followed by** than.

> He drives *more rapidly than* the speed limit permits.
> I arrived *sooner than* anybody else.

**The adverbs** bad **and** well **have irregular comparatives:** bad-worse **and** well-better.

> He reads Spanish *better than* French.
> I feel *worse than* yesterday.

*Write the comparative form of the adverbs in parentheses. Include the word* than.

1.  We arrived at the party (late) they.                    *later than*
2.  We will get there (soon) you.                           _____
3.  He spoke (loudly) usual.                                _____
4.  She answered me (quickly) I expected.                   _____
5.  She plays the piano (well) her sister.                  _____
6.  She also sings (beautifully) her sister.                _____
7.  The train arrived (late) ever before.                   _____
8.  You can run (fast) I.                                    _____
9.  We speak much (slowly) the teacher.                     _____
10. Sue prepares her homework (carefully) I do.             _____
11. Yvonne works (hard) the other students.                 _____
12. I get up every morning (lazily) Hector.                 _____
13. You speak English much (well) I.                        _____
14. He can do the work (easily) I.                          _____
15. She returned (soon) we expected.                        _____
16. He goes there (often) I.                                _____

**The superlative of one-syllable adjectives is formed by adding** est.

| | |
|---|---|
| warm-warmest | high-highest |
| big-biggest | hot-hottest |

**The superlative of adjectives with more than one syllable is usually made by using** most.

| | |
|---|---|
| interesting-most interesting | difficult-most difficult |
| beautiful-most beautiful | expensive-most expensive |

**However, two-syllable adjectives that end in** y **or** ow **add** est. **The** y **is changed to** i **before the** est **is added.**

| | |
|---|---|
| heavy-heaviest | narrow-narrowest |
| sleepy-sleepiest | deadly-deadliest |

**The superlatives of** good **and** bad **are irregular:** good-best **and** bad-worst.

| |
|---|
| He uses the *best* mechanic in town. |
| I had the *worst* grade in the class. |

*Write the superlative form of the adjective. Be sure to use the word the.*

1.  Joy is (tall) girl in our class.                              *the tallest*
2.  She is (athletic) student in the school.           _____
3.  New York is (large) city in the United States.           _____
4.  Alice is (intelligent) girl in our class.           _____
5.  Carlo is (good) student in our class.           _____
6.  The Mississippi River is (long) river in the United States. _____
7.  August is (hot) month of the year in the United States.           _____
8.  This exercise is (difficult) one in the whole book.           _____
9.  Park Avenue is (wide) street in New York City.           _____
10.  Mr. Gilbert is (busy) teacher in our school.           _____
11.  Grace is (friendly) girl in our group.           _____
12.  Miss Rice is (good) teacher of English in our school.           _____
13.  That store is (large) store in town.           _____
14.  He is (bad) student in our class.           _____
15.  January is (cold) month of the year in the United States.           _____

## mistakes of fact 3

*The items in boldface are mistakes. Change them to make the facts correct, and write your answers in the blanks.*

1. The capital of the United States is **Philadelphia.**     *Washington*
2. The Atlantic Ocean lies **south** of the United States. _____
3. The opposite of *cheap* is **poor.** _____
4. In the word *knife*, the letter **n** is silent (not pronounced). _____
5. The past tense form of *can* is **might.** _____
6. The past tense form of *speak* is **spoken.** _____
7. There are **fifty** seconds in a minute. _____
8. On a watch or clock, the minute hand is **shorter** than the hour hand. _____
9. The English alphabet has **twenty-four** letters. _____
10. The superlative form of the adjective *good* is **better.** _____
11. The first president of the United States was **Abraham Lincoln.** _____
12. There are **two** feet in a yard. _____
13. There are ten millimeters in one **decimeter.** _____
14. Mexico lies **north** of the United States. _____
15. We pronounce the word *stopped* as a word of **two syllables.** _____
16. We pronounce the word *wanted* as a word of **one syllable.** _____
17. We accent the word *auditorium* on the **second** syllable. _____
18. April is the **fifth** month of the year. _____
19. To *call up* someone is to **criticize** him or her. _____
20. People see with their **ears.** _____
21. In the United States, the coldest season of the year is **summer.** _____
22. Abraham Lincoln was president of the United States during the **Revolutionary War.** _____

*Write the past tense of the following verbs.*

| | | | | | |
|---|---|---|---|---|---|
| 1. go | *went* | 23. come | _____ | 45. want | _____ |
| 2. need | _____ | 24. shut | _____ | 46. give | _____ |
| 3. take | _____ | 25. shake | _____ | 47. get | _____ |
| 4. teach | _____ | 26. sell | _____ | 48. forget | _____ |
| 5. tell | _____ | 27. see | _____ | 49. find | _____ |
| 6. think | _____ | 28. ring | _____ | 50. fight | _____ |
| 7. hear | _____ | 29. ride | _____ | 51. feel | _____ |
| 8. write | _____ | 30. read | _____ | 52. eat | _____ |
| 9. count | _____ | 31. put | _____ | 53. drive | _____ |
| 10. have | _____ | 32. visit | _____ | 54. drink | _____ |
| 11. prepare | _____ | 33. study | _____ | 55. do | _____ |
| 12. work | _____ | 34. live | _____ | 56. cut | _____ |
| 13. sweep | _____ | 35. meet | _____ | 57. cost | _____ |
| 14. steal | _____ | 36. mean | _____ | 58. catch | _____ |
| 15. stand | _____ | 37. make | _____ | 59. buy | _____ |
| 16. sleep | _____ | 38. lose | _____ | 60. spring | _____ |
| 17. paint | _____ | 39. leave | _____ | 61. break | _____ |
| 18. push | _____ | 40. know | _____ | 62. blow | _____ |
| 19. pull | _____ | 41. keep | _____ | 63. begin | _____ |
| 20. weep | _____ | 42. be | _____ | 64. become | _____ |
| 21. sit | _____ | 43. like | _____ | 65. start | _____ |
| 22. sing | _____ | 44. hit | _____ | 66. stop | _____ |

*Select the correct answer and write it in the space provided.*

1. The opposite of *sharp* is (new, bright, old, dull).                    *dull*

2. We pronounce the contraction *he'll* to rhyme with
   (fell, fill, feel, fall).                                                _____

3. Which of these verbs is in the past tense:
   see, feel, fight, got, wait?                                             _____

4. Which of these verbs is in the present tense:
   gave, went, had, know, found?                                           _____

5. Which of these verbs has the same form in the past tense
   as in the present tense: go, hit, find, get, tell?                      _____

6. Which two of the following words are both opposites
   of *right*: easy, wrong, straight, left, soon?                          _____

7. *Right away* means (later, immediately, often, to the right).           _____

8. To *pick out* a thing is to (need, want, choose, lose) it.              _____

9. In which one of these words do we pronounce the
   letter *s* like *z*: miss, this, is, pass?                              _____

10. In which of these four seasons of the year does it rain
    most often in the United States:
    spring, summer, fall, winter?                                          _____

11. We pronounce the contraction *we're* to rhyme with
    (her, where, hear, wore).                                              _____

12. The word *composition* has four syllables. On which
    syllable do we accent the word—on the first, second,
    third, or fourth syllable?                                             _____

13. We use the word *hard* as the opposite of
    (good, new, soft, fine).                                               _____

14. The auxiliary verb that we use to form the future
    tense is (do, does, can, will, did).                                   _____

15. Which of these past tense forms do we pronounce as a
    word of one syllable: wanted, needed, walked, pointed?                 _____

16. Which of these past tense forms do we pronounce as a
    word of two syllables: pulled, asked, placed, talked,
    wanted?                                                                _____

*Write the correct prepositions or particles in the blanks.*

1. The leaves fall _____ the trees in October.     *from*
2. What is the reason _____ the delay?     _____
3. It is dark in this room. Please turn _____ the light.     _____
4. Hurry! Martha is waiting _____ us.     _____
5. All the students are laughing _____ us.     _____
6. _____ present, he is the best student in the class.     _____
7. Noriko was absent _____ class yesterday.     _____
8. What are they talking _____?     _____
9. What is he laughing _____?     _____
10. What are you shouting _____?     _____
11. The beggar asked me _____ some money.     _____
12. Hurry! We will be late _____ class.     _____
13. She spends a lot of money _____ travel.     _____
14. This pen belongs _____ Mr. Abrams.     _____
15. I always go to school _____ bus.     _____
16. I spoke to her _____ the telephone yesterday.     _____
17. The airplane flew directly _____ our house.     _____
18. The child ran and tried to hide _____ the tree.     _____
19. He tried to explain _____ me what he wanted.     _____
20. Esther is looking _____ the book that she lost.     _____
21. Did you find _____ what Patrick wanted?     _____
22. He is leaving _____ New York from Gatwick.     _____
23. Ellen lives directly _____ the street from us.     _____
24. Subways travel _____ the ground.     _____
25. What is the difference _____ those two words?     _____

*Select the correct form. Write your answers in the blanks.*

1. Listen! Someone (knocks, is knocking) at the door.  *is knocking*
2. (That, Those) books belong to Tina.  _____
3. Angela didn't like the movie (also, either).  _____
4. I (can, could) not come to the lesson yesterday.  _____
5. I saw (they, them) in the cafeteria at noon.  _____
6. (No, Not) one student was absent from class this morning.  _____
7. Marie is taller (as, than) Trudy.  _____
8. This pen (belong, belongs) to Rose.  _____
9. Does Jean (speak, speaks) English well?  _____
10. Helen plays the piano very (good, well).  _____
11. She also sings (beautiful, beautifully).  _____
12. Do you want (a, an) apple?  _____
13. We waited (a, an) hour for him.  _____
14. We also waited (a, an) whole hour for Jim.  _____
15. He spends (much, many) time on his homework.  _____
16. (Was, Were) Diane and her sister at the party last night?  _____
17. He is the man (who, which) came to see you.  _____
18. There (was, were) three students absent from class today.  _____
19. Dick always prepares his lessons (careful, carefully).  _____
20. She sings very (good, well).  _____
21. He wants (go, to go) to the movies with us tonight.  _____
22. It was difficult (learn, to learn) so many new words.  _____
23. What time (do, did) you get up this morning?  _____
24. He cannot (speak, to speak) English well.  _____

Some *is used in affirmative sentences.*

> Andy brought *some* friends to the party.

Any *is used in negative sentences.*

> Andy didn't see *any* friends at the party.

*Select the correct form. Write your answers in the blanks.*

1.  There aren't (some, any) chairs in the room.                                          *any*
2.  I saw (some, any) cars in the street.                                                 _____
3.  I didn't see (some, any).                                                             _____
4.  I have (some, any) new magazines with me.                                             _____
5.  He says that he saw (some, any) police officers on the corner.                        _____
6.  I don't believe that he saw (some, any).                                              _____
7.  I don't have (some, any) time to study English.                                       _____
8.  I wrote (some, any) letters to them last night.                                       _____
9.  There are (some, any) flowers in the vase.                                            _____
10. There aren't (some, any) flowers in this vase.                                        _____
11. She says that she put (some, any) water in the vase.                                  _____
12. I didn't see her put (some, any) water in the vase.                                   _____
13. I gave Tom (some, any) money to buy the tickets.                                      _____
14. He never makes (some, any) mistakes in grammar.                                       _____
15. I learned (some, any) new words in English in today's lesson.                         _____
16. Maybe you learned some, but I didn't learn (some, any).                               _____
17. There were (some, any) pretty pictures on the wall.                                   _____
18. I didn't see (some, any) pretty pictures there.                                        _____
19. She has (some, any) very famous clients.                                              _____
20. However, she says that she doesn't have (some, any) famous clients.                   _____
21. The teacher taught us (some, any) important grammar rules.                            _____

**The words** someone, somebody, something, somewhere **are used in affirmative sentences.**

> I heard her whisper *something* to you.

**The words** anyone, anybody, anything, and anywhere **are used in negative sentences.**

> I didn't see *anybody* I knew in the room.

*Select the correct form. Write your answers in the blanks.*

1. She didn't say (something, anything) to me about it.     *anything*
2. He told me (something, anything) about his trip.     _____
3. There is (something, anything) wrong with this.     _____
4. I don't see (something, anything) wrong with it.     _____
5. She lives (somewhere, anywhere) on Sunset Boulevard.     _____
6. I can't find my pen (somewhere, anywhere).     _____
7. I hear (someone, anyone) in the next room.     _____
8. I don't hear (someone, anyone).     _____
9. I saw (someone, anyone) in the hall with Tony.     _____
10. There isn't (someone, anyone) at the door.     _____
11. I was sure that I heard (someone, anyone) at the door.     _____
12. She told me (something, anything) about the new teacher.     _____
13. She didn't say (something, anything) to me about her.     _____
14. I left my books (somewhere, anywhere) in this room.     _____
15. Now I can't find them (somewhere, anywhere).     _____
16. They say that there is (something, anything) wrong with the elevator.     _____
17. There wasn't (something, anything) wrong with it a few minutes ago when I used it.     _____
18. The doctors gave me (something, anything) for my cough.     _____
19. I hear (somebody, anybody) in Ms. Canetti's office.     _____
20. I'm sure there isn't (somebody, anybody) there.     _____
21. There isn't (somebody, anybody) who can help him now.     _____

## opposites 3

*Write the opposites of the following words.*

| | | | | | |
|---|---|---|---|---|---|
| 1. | sweet | *sour* | 25. | tall | _____ |
| 2. | young | _____ | 26. | few | _____ |
| 3. | buy | _____ | 27. | clean | _____ |
| 4. | often | _____ | 28. | absent | _____ |
| 5. | beautiful | _____ | 29. | pull | _____ |
| 6. | loose | _____ | 30. | easy | _____ |
| 7. | high | _____ | 31. | narrow | _____ |
| 8. | laugh | _____ | 32. | remember | _____ |
| 9. | dangerous | _____ | 33. | smooth | _____ |
| 10. | inside | _____ | 34. | low | _____ |
| 11. | hard | _____ | 35. | in front of | _____ |
| 12. | dull | _____ | 36. | cold | _____ |
| 13. | happy | _____ | 37. | in | _____ |
| 14. | push | _____ | 38. | winter | _____ |
| 15. | wide | _____ | 39. | good | _____ |
| 16. | careful | _____ | 40. | east | _____ |
| 17. | empty | _____ | 41. | sour | _____ |
| 18. | white | _____ | 42. | soft | _____ |
| 19. | thick | _____ | 43. | summer | _____ |
| 20. | stop | _____ | 44. | late | _____ |
| 21. | behind | _____ | 45. | dark | _____ |
| 22. | expensive | _____ | 46. | down | _____ |
| 23. | take | _____ | 47. | sit | _____ |
| 24. | thin | _____ | 48. | big | _____ |

For each of the words below, write the consonant which is written but not pronounced.

| | | | | | |
|---|---|---|---|---|---|
| 1. | write | *w* | 22. | knee | _____ |
| 2. | listen | _____ | 23. | walk | _____ |
| 3. | knock | _____ | 24. | talk | _____ |
| 4. | knew | _____ | 25. | kneel | _____ |
| 5. | often | _____ | 26. | Wednesday | _____ |
| 6. | honest | _____ | 27. | wrong | _____ |
| 7. | whole | _____ | 28. | should | _____ |
| 8. | whistle | _____ | 29. | wrist | _____ |
| 9. | dumb | _____ | 30. | sign | _____ |
| 10. | half | _____ | 31. | sword | _____ |
| 11. | knife | _____ | 32. | knit | _____ |
| 12. | could | _____ | 33. | aisle | _____ |
| 13. | Christmas | _____ | 34. | numb | _____ |
| 14. | island | _____ | 35. | scissors | _____ |
| 15. | answer | _____ | 36. | scene | _____ |
| 16. | doubt | _____ | 37. | ghost | _____ |
| 17. | gnaw | _____ | 38. | wrote | _____ |
| 18. | climb | _____ | 39. | czar | _____ |
| 19. | debt | _____ | 40. | pneumonia | _____ |
| 20. | thumb | _____ | 41. | knot | _____ |
| 21. | honor | _____ | 42. | align | _____ |

*Study and memorize the past tense forms of the following irregular verbs.*

| build | built | lend | lent | shoot | shot |
|-------|-------|------|------|-------|------|
| fly   | flew  | pay  | paid | spend | spent |
| grow  | grew  | run  | ran  | throw | threw |
| hold  | held  | say  | said | wear  | wore |
| hurt  | hurt  | send | sent | win   | won |

*Write the correct past tense form of the verbs in parentheses.*

1.  Mr. Ovando (fly) to Chicago last week.                                      *flew*
2.  Who (lend) him the money to buy the car?                                    _____
3.  The child (run) and hid behind a tree.                                      _____
4.  During our vacation last summer, we (spend) two weeks in Paris.             _____
5.  These flowers (grow) in my garden.                                          _____
6.  The police officer (shoot) the man in the arm.                              _____
7.  The teacher became angry and (throw) our compositions into the wastepaper basket.   _____
8.  Brigitte fell and (hurt) her arm.                                           _____
9.  I (pay) ten dollars for my English book.                                    _____
10. Paolo (say) that he was too busy to go with us.                             _____
11. Grace (wear) a long white dress to the party.                               _____
12. They (send) us several presents from Mexico last summer.                    _____
13. The woman (hold) the child's arm tightly as they crossed the street.        _____
14. We played tennis yesterday, and John (win) every game.                      _____
15. She was born in Italy but (grow) up in the United States.                   _____
16. The six police officers easily (hold) back the crowd.                       _____
17. Ray (run) away from home when he was only ten years old.                    _____
18. At the sound of the gun, all the birds (fly) away.                          _____
19. We (send) him two letters last week.                                        _____
20. Dolores angrily (throw) the money on the floor.                             _____

Very *means there is a lot of something.*

> The car is *very* long, but it fits into the space.

Too *means an excess of something; there is more of something than is necessary or than we can use.*

> The car is *too* long. It will not fit into the space.

*Write* too *or* very *in the spaces provided.*

1. I cannot wear this ring because it is _____ small for my finger.                                    *too*

2. This magazine is _____ large, but it will go into my desk drawer.                                    _____

3. That other magazine, however, is _____ large to go into my desk drawer.                             _____

4. That chair is _____ heavy for Sue. She cannot pick it up.                                            _____

5. It is a _____ heavy chair, but Nora is strong and can easily pick it up.                             _____

6. You are speaking _____ fast. I cannot understand you.     _____

7. Our teacher speaks _____ fast, but I always understand her.                                          _____

8. This soup is _____ hot. I cannot eat it.                 _____

9. The weather in Canada is _____ cold in winter, but Mr. Soto enjoys it very much.                     _____

10. I cannot go out now. It is raining _____ hard.          _____

11. The sun was _____ hot for the child, and she became sick.                                           _____

12. It is _____ late, but if we hurry we can still catch the train.                                     _____

13. Betty says that she is _____ tired to go for a walk.    _____

14. The doctor says that Bill is still _____ weak to go to work.                                        _____

15. Frank studies English _____ hard and is making good progress.                                       _____

**When we add** ed *to a verb that ends in a voiceless consonant (such as p, t, f, k, s, sh), the* ed *is pronounced like* t.

| | |
|---|---|
| ask*ed* | pass*ed* |
| walk*ed* | push*ed* |

**When we add** ed *to a verb that ends in a vowel or in a voiced consonant (such as b, d, v, g, z), the* ed *is pronounced like* d.

| | |
|---|---|
| chang*ed* | sneez*ed* |
| grabb*ed* | liv*ed* |

*Write* t *or* d *to show the pronunciation of the* ed *in each word.*

| | | | | | |
|---|---|---|---|---|---|
| 1. | pulled | *d* | 22. | crossed | _____ |
| 2. | walked | *t* | 23. | earned | _____ |
| 3. | passed | _____ | 24. | entered | _____ |
| 4. | washed | _____ | 25. | stopped | _____ |
| 5. | closed | _____ | 26. | saved | _____ |
| 6. | changed | _____ | 27. | knocked | _____ |
| 7. | used | _____ | 28. | lived | _____ |
| 8. | liked | _____ | 29. | killed | _____ |
| 9. | picked | _____ | 30. | played | _____ |
| 10. | mailed | _____ | 31. | showed | _____ |
| 11. | excused | _____ | 32. | dropped | _____ |
| 12. | boiled | _____ | 33. | turned | _____ |
| 13. | finished | _____ | 34. | looked | _____ |
| 14. | burned | _____ | 35. | smoked | _____ |
| 15. | filled | _____ | 36. | wished | _____ |
| 16. | poured | _____ | 37. | hurried | _____ |
| 17. | worked | _____ | 38. | rushed | _____ |
| 18. | studied | _____ | 39. | placed | _____ |
| 19. | talked | _____ | 40. | jumped | _____ |
| 20. | spelled | _____ | 41. | remained | _____ |
| 21. | thanked | _____ | 42. | arrived | _____ |

*Change the words in the italics to the contracted form.*

1. *I am* very busy today.        *I'm*
2. *You are* a very good student.        _____
3. *He is* going to the movies with us.        _____
4. *She is* also going with us.        _____
5. *They are* both good students.        _____
6. *I will* meet you at six o'clock.        _____
7. *You will* get tired if you walk so far.        _____
8. *He will* be back at six o'clock.        _____
9. *He will* be here soon.        _____
10. *We have* been to London.        _____
11. *She has* seen the Tower of London.        _____
12. I *do not* know her well.        _____
13. She *does not* speak English well.        _____
14. He *did not* speak to me about it.        _____
15. They *did not* arrive on time for the lesson.        _____
16. I *will not* be back until three o'clock.        _____
17. Kathy *will not* be able to meet us.        _____
18. I *cannot* go to the party tonight.        _____
19. She *is not* a good student.        _____
20. They *are not* going to the party with us.        _____
21. Sally *was not* at the meeting last night.        _____
22. Angela and Anita *were not* at the meeting, either.        _____
23. *There is* someone at the door.        _____
24. *I am* not going to the movie tonight.        _____

*Change the following contractions to the full form.*

1. He *doesn't* speak English well.        *does not*
2. I *can't* meet you after the lesson.  _____
3. I *don't* know her very well.  _____
4. He *won't* be back until later.  _____
5. *She's* a good student.  _____
6. *It's* a very hot day.  _____
7. *She'll* be back in an hour.  _____
8. *They're* the best students in our class.  _____
9. *It'll* be easy for you to find him.  _____
10. *She's* a very nice girl.  _____
11. He *won't* be able to go with us.  _____
12. Yuriko *wasn't* able to telephone her parents.  _____
13. *I'm* leaving on the three o'clock train.  _____
14. *He's* going to study French next year.  _____
15. I *didn't* have time to call you last night.  _____
16. They *aren't* going to the movie with us.  _____
17. She *isn't* a good student.  _____
18. They *weren't* at the meeting either.  _____
19. *There's* only one really good student in our class.  _____
20. *There'll* be plenty of room for everyone.  _____
21. He *doesn't* have much money with him.  _____
22. They *don't* have many friends in this town.  _____
23. *You're* going to be late for class.  _____
24. *You'll* be tired after so much work.  _____

*Write the word that rhymes with the contractions given.*

1.  I'm: him, ham, time, some          *time*
2.  she's: miss, place, sneeze, this      _____
3.  you're: four, tore, fear, sure      _____
4.  I've: leave, prove, five, save      _____
5.  they've: five, leave, save, prove      _____
6.  it's: eats, sits, sets, fights      _____
7.  we're: were, wear, hear, her      _____
8.  they're: fear, hair, wire, four      _____
9.  I'll: will, mile, meal, call      _____
10. you'll: full, feel, jewel, fell      _____
11. he'll: well, will, hole, feel      _____
12. can't: paint, pant, faint, pint      _____
13. there's: wears, fears, pours, cheers      _____
14. they'll: wheel, well, jail, will      _____
15. he's: this, his, freeze, police      _____
16. you've: prove, love, save, wave      _____
17. it'll: will, little, tell, whistle      _____
18. we'll: well, fill, fell, wheel      _____
19. she'll: shell, shall, will, meal      _____
20. we've: prove, leave, left, love      _____

*Write the correct prepositions in the blanks.*

1. She place the accent _____ the wrong syllable.      *on*
2. English grammar is very easy _____ me.      _____
3. The child ran _____ his mother.      _____
4. This book belongs _____ Gil.      _____
5. He told us all _____ his trip to Europe.      _____
6. She will be in Europe _____ six months.      _____
7. I'll be back _____ ten minutes.      _____
8. I can study during the day but not _____ night.      _____
9. Tom prefers to study _____ the morning.      _____
10. He wants to take a trip _____ the world.      _____
11. We need more practice _____ conversation.      _____
12. She must spend more time _____ her English.      _____
13. They played a trick _____ him.      _____
14. Later they all laughed _____ him.      _____
15. He makes many mistakes _____ spelling.      _____
16. I saw the president _____ television last night.      _____
17. Debbie wants to borrow some money _____ me.      _____
18. Shall I lend it _____ her?      _____
19. He arrived _____ Washington yesterday.      _____
20. The doctor gave me some medicine _____ my cough.      _____
21. We went _____ a walk in the park.      _____
22. She left a message _____ you.      _____
23. He will leave _____ Wednesday for New York.      _____
24. She will be very angry _____ you.      _____

# 101 Vocabulary review 4

*Select the correct answer and write it in the space provided.*

1. The opposite of *cheap* is (poor, expensive, new, old).    *expensive*

2. Which of these verbs is in the past tense:
   see, fly, grow, ran, wear? _____

3. We pronounce the word *said* to rhyme with
   (paid, head, sad, hid). _____

4. Which of these verbs is in the present tense:
   threw, held, lent, shot, send? _____

5. Which of these verbs has the same form in the past tense
   as in the present tense: lend, send, hurt, win? _____

6. *Pretty good* means (very good, not good,
   rather good, awfully good). _____

7. If you feel too hot, what do you do with your coat:
   put it on, take it off, pick it up, put it away? _____

8. What is the superlative form of the adjective *good*? _____

9. What is the superlative form of the adjective *bad*? _____

10. Which one of these past tense forms do we pronounce
    as a word of only one syllable: painted, counted, pushed,
    wanted? _____

11. Which one of these past tense forms do we pronounce
    as a word of two syllables: pulled, asked, thanked,
    waited, rained? _____

12. Which of the following do we call a contracted form:
    you are, he is, we'll, they were? _____

13. We pronounce the contraction *she'll* to rhyme with
    (tell, tall, still, steal). _____

14. In which of these can you travel fastest:
    streetcar, bus, train, airplane? _____

15. Which one of the following words is not spelled correctly:
    telephone, Wednesday, sylable, stopping, January? _____

16. Which letter in the word *wrist* is silent (not pronounced)? _____

17. Which letter in the word *ghost* is silent (not pronounced)? _____

*Select the correct form. Write your answers in the blanks.*

1. The book, (which, who) is very old, is for sale.   *which*
2. She is much taller (as, than) Rita.   _____
3. I didn't see (someone, anyone) in the room.   _____
4. Listen! It (rains, is raining).   _____
5. Yesterday he (feel, felt) much better.   _____
6. They have (many, much) friends in Washington.   _____
7. Do you put (much, many) sugar in your coffee?   _____
8. She doesn't want to study French next year (also, either).   _____
9. What time (will you, you will) be able to meet me?   _____
10. We (are going, go) to school every day by bus.   _____
11. They (have, are having) their lunch now.   _____
12. (This, These) pencils belong to Rachel.   _____
13. Were you absent (in, from) school yesterday?   _____
14. Let's not (to eat, eat) in that restaurant again.   _____
15. The child (run, ran) from the room.   _____
16. I'm sorry, but I (can, could) not come to class yesterday.   _____
17. Listen! The telephone (rings, is ringing).   _____
18. Does he (makes, make) many mistakes in spelling?   _____
19. What time (did, do) you get up this morning?   _____
20. There (was, were) many students absent from class yesterday.   _____
21. It is difficult (understand, to understand) him.   _____
22. Nancy always prepares her lessons (careful, carefully).   _____
23. Dennis speaks English (good, well).   _____
24. I waited for him for (a, an) hour.   _____

# 103 Ordinal numbers

*We use ordinal numbers for names of streets, for dates, and to show sequence. The ordinal numbers for 1, 2, 3, and 5 have irregular forms. All other ordinal numbers are formed by adding* th *to the cardinal number. Some of these ordinal numbers, however, require spelling changes, as in* twelfth *and* twentieth.

| Cardinal Number | Ordinal Number | Abbreviated Form |
|---|---|---|
| 1 | first | 1st |
| 2 | second | 2nd |
| 3 | third | 3rd |
| 4 | fourth | 4th |
| 5 | fifth | 5th |
| 6 | sixth | 6th |

*Write the ordinal numbers and their abbreviations.*

| | Ordinal Number | Abbreviated Form |
|---|---|---|
| 1. one | first | 1st |
| 2. two | second | 2nd |
| 3. three | _____ | _____ |
| 4. four | _____ | _____ |
| 5. five | _____ | _____ |
| 6. six | _____ | _____ |
| 7. seven | _____ | _____ |
| 8. eight | _____ | _____ |
| 9. nine | _____ | _____ |
| 10. ten | _____ | _____ |
| 11. eleven | _____ | _____ |
| 12. twelve | _____ | _____ |
| 13. thirteen | _____ | _____ |
| 14. eighteen | _____ | _____ |
| 15. twenty | _____ | _____ |
| 16. twenty-one | _____ | _____ |
| 17. twenty-five | _____ | _____ |
| 18. thirty | _____ | _____ |

**Some general rules to remember in forming the negatives follow.**

**a.** To be, **present and past tenses**
**Form the negative by placing** not **after the verb.**

> I am *not* a good tennis player.    There were *not* surprised to see me.

**b. Auxiliary verb**
**Form the negative by placing** not **after the auxiliary.**

> She will *not* take the computer    You may *not* go out this late.
> classes.

**c.** Do, does, did
**Form the negative with the auxiliaries** do, does, **and** did **by placing** not **after the auxiliaries.**

> We do *not* speak Chinese.    He did *not* win first place.

*Change to the negative form. Write the complete verb in the blanks.*

1. They will study in our class.                          *will not study*
2. She speaks English well.                               _____
3. She spoke to me in English.                            _____
4. She can speak English well.                            _____
5. He is an excellent student.                            _____
6. They went with us to the movies last night.            _____
7. Henry was in class yesterday.                          _____
8. They are having their lunch now.                       _____
9. It is raining hard.                                    _____
10. The telephone is ringing.                             _____
11. The wind blows hard at this time of year.             _____
12. I will be back in an hour.                            _____
13. He brought his sister to the lesson.                  _____
14. She plays the piano very well.                        _____
15. We must tell Mr. Perez about this.                    _____
16. You may wait here.                                    _____
17. He wrote his composition in pencil.                   _____
18. It is a very warm day.                                _____

# 105 Review: question form

**Some general rules to follow when forming questions follow.**

**a.** To be, **present and past tenses**

**Form the question by placing the verb before the subject.**

> *Are you* his friend?    *Was he* interested in the stereo?

**b.  Auxiliary verb**

**Form the question by placing the auxiliary verb before the subject.**

> *May we* go to the movies with you?    *Will she* win first prize?

**c.**  Do, does, did

**The auxiliaries** do, does, **and** did **are used for questions where there is no regular auxiliary verb.**

> She has a lot of friends here.    *Does she* have a lot of friends here?
> You left early.    *Did you* leave early?

*Change to the question form. Write the complete verb and subject in the blanks.*

1.   They will return on Monday.  *Will they return*
2.   He left on the five o'clock train.  _____
3.   She is a good manager.  _____
4.   They visited us in our home last night.  _____
5.   He will be out of town for a week.  _____
6.   Someone is knocking at the door.  _____
7.   They were not in class yesterday.  _____
8.   Rudy was sick yesterday.  _____
9.   We are going to study French next year.  _____
10.  It is going to rain.  _____
11.  There is someone at the door.  _____
12.  He spoke to her about it.  _____
13.  She speaks English perfectly.  _____
14.  Patricia is one of his best friends.  _____
15.  They study in the same class.  _____
16.  She can meet us after the lesson.  _____
17.  We must write our exercises in ink.  _____

Write the number of syllables in each of the words below. Then show which syllable is stressed in each word. Practice pronouncing each word.

| | Number of Syllables | Stressed Syllable |
|---|---|---|
| 1. apartment | *3* | *2nd* |
| 2. Canada | | |
| 3. repair | | |
| 4. banana | | |
| 5. cafeteria | | |
| 6. Mississippi | | |
| 7. Chicago | | |
| 8. popular | | |
| 9. popularity | | |
| 10. population | | |
| 11. capital | | |
| 12. telephone | | |
| 13. tomorrow | | |
| 14. president | | |
| 15. preparation | | |
| 16. prohibited | | |
| 17. excused | | |
| 18. finished | | |
| 19. library | | |
| 20. Saturday | | |
| 21. Wednesday | | |
| 22. nationality | | |
| 23. language | | |
| 24. holiday | | |

# 107 Regular and irregular verbs

*Write* reg *beside each regular verb. Write* irreg *beside each irregular verb. If you do not remember all the verbs, check previous lessons.*

| | | | | | |
|---|---|---|---|---|---|
| 1. | sit | *irreg* | 23. | stand | _____ |
| 2. | wait | *reg* | 24. | need | _____ |
| 3. | bring | _____ | 25. | speak | _____ |
| 4. | count | _____ | 26. | meet | _____ |
| 5. | wish | _____ | 27. | talk | _____ |
| 6. | write | _____ | 28. | thank | _____ |
| 7. | win | _____ | 29. | make | _____ |
| 8. | wear | _____ | 30. | study | _____ |
| 9. | wash | _____ | 31. | stop | _____ |
| 10. | want | _____ | 32. | send | _____ |
| 11. | walk | _____ | 33. | shake | _____ |
| 12. | throw | _____ | 34. | run | _____ |
| 13. | think | _____ | 35. | raise | _____ |
| 14. | tell | _____ | 36. | put | _____ |
| 15. | turn | _____ | 37. | remain | _____ |
| 16. | visit | _____ | 38. | bring | _____ |
| 17. | use | _____ | 39. | protect | _____ |
| 18. | teach | _____ | 40. | pass | _____ |
| 19. | take | _____ | 41. | pick | _____ |
| 20. | swim | _____ | 42. | buy | _____ |
| 21. | call | _____ | 43. | play | _____ |
| 22. | understand | _____ | 44. | cut | _____ |

# 108 Abbreviations

*Write the full form of the items which appear below.*

1. 6 oz.    *six ounces*
2. 1 lb.    _____
3. 1 mi.    _____
4. 7 A.M.   _____
5. 6 P.M.   _____
6. .5       _____
7. 1/2      _____
8. 1/4      _____
9. 6%       _____
10. #5      _____
11. 68°     _____
12. AC      _____
13. DC      _____
14. etc.    _____
15. 1 gal.  _____
16. TV      _____
17. C.O.D.  _____
18. qt.     _____
19. pt.     _____
20. yd.     _____
21. in.     _____
22. &       _____
23. Inc.    _____
24. 2 yrs.  _____

25. 4 ft.     _____
26. 7th St.   _____
27. Ave.      _____
28. Blvd.     _____
29. Rd.       _____
30. Bldg.     _____
31. Feb.      _____
32. Aug.      _____
33. Dec.      _____
34. sq. ft.   _____
35. 1st       _____
36. 3rd       _____
37. 7th       _____
38. Thurs.    _____
39. Wed.      _____
40. FM        _____
41. NBC       _____
42. NY        _____
43. PA        _____
44. D.C.      _____
45. MD        _____
46. MI        _____
47. CA        _____
48. IL        _____

*Write the correct prepositions in the blanks.*

1. She came to this country _____ 1984.                                    *in*
2. He goes to his country house _____ bus.                                 _____
3. She lived _____ home until she was eighteen.                            _____
4. There is someone _____ the door.                                        _____
5. She studied French _____ two years.                                     _____
6. I spoke _____ him about it.                                             _____
7. Please explain _____ me what you mean.                                  _____
8. I looked everywhere _____ my book.                                      _____
9. We all went _____ a walk in the park.                                   _____
10. This chair is too heavy _____ me to carry.                             _____
11. In tennis, the ball goes _____ the net.                                _____
12. We drove to school _____ John's new car.                               _____
13. She stole the money _____ her friend.                                  _____
14. The sun rises _____ the east.                                          _____
15. He makes many mistakes _____ grammar.                                  _____
16. I often go to their home _____ dinner.                                 _____
17. I'll be back _____ an hour.                                            _____
18. I am sure that I can finish this work _____ a few hours.  _____
19. Does the train always arrive _____ time?                               _____
20. She visited us _____ two weeks.                                        _____
21. John went to California _____ plane.                                   _____
22. He telephoned me _____ the middle of the night.                        _____
23. She opened the door and walked _____ the room.                         _____
24. The rock fell _____ the river.                                         _____

## mistakes of fact 4

*The items in boldface are mistakes. Change them to make the facts correct, and write your answers in the blanks.*

1. December is the **first** month of the year.    *last*
2. The next-to-the-last month of the year is **October.**    _____
3. The word *cafeteria* has **four** syllables.    _____
4. We accent the word *cafeteria* on the **fourth** syllable.    _____
5. The contracted form of *will not* is **willn't.**    _____
6. The past tense form of *cut* is **caught.**    _____
7. The past tense form of *hit* is **heat.**    _____
8. The largest state in the United States is **Florida.**    _____
9. Canada lies **east** of the United States.    ____ ____
10. The plural form of *that* is **these.**    ____ ____
11. There are **four** feet in a yard.    _____
12. There are **six** quarts in a gallon.    _____
13. There are **one hundred** millimeters in one centimeter.    _____
14. There are **fourteen** inches in a foot.    _____
15. The second largest city in the United States is **Philadelphia.**    _____
16. The longest river in the United States is the **Hudson River.**    _____
17. The people of Brazil speak **Spanish.**    _____
18. We pronounce the word *thanked* as a word of **two syllables.**    _____
19. The coldest season of the year in the United States is **autumn.**    _____
20. If today is Tuesday, then the day before yesterday was **Saturday.**    _____
21. If today is Tuesday, then the day after tomorrow will be **Friday.**    _____
22. There are **fifty-six** weeks in a year.    _____
23. In the United States, we celebrate Independence Day on **May 30th.**    _____

*Select the correct answer and write it in the space provided.*

1. Which one of these verbs is in the past tense: see, bring, find, won, say?  *won*

2. Which one of these verbs has the same form in the past tense as in the present tense: win, hit, take, sit, see?  _____

3. A synonym for *plaything* is (lesson, toy, classroom, chalk). _____

4. To *call on* someone is to (see, telephone, visit, like) him or her.  _____

5. If I am *tired out*, I am (rather tired, not tired, very tired, a little tired).  _____

6. Which one of these words is not spelled correctly: daughter, grammer, interesting, secretary, Philadelphia?  _____

7. In order to *sweep*, you need a (hammer, gun, stick, broom).  _____

8. We pronounce the contraction *we're* to rhyme with (there, wear, near, fare, wire).  _____

9. The opposite of *in front of* is (near, alongside, behind, between).  _____

10. Which letter in the word *half* is silent (not pronounced)? _____

11. Which letter in the word *walk* is silent (not pronounced)?_____

12. In which of these words do we pronounce the letter *s* like *z*: kiss, visit, pass, ask?  _____

13. Which word does not rhyme with the others: lie, high, cry, fly, tea, buy?  _____

14. Which word does not rhyme with the others: fight, bite, right, height, weight?  _____

15. A synonym for *cent* is (nickel, dime, penny, quarter).  _____

16. We pronounce the word *lose* to rhyme with (chose, rose, choose, blouse).  _____

17. A synonym for *at last* is (later, once, finally, immediately)._____

*Select the correct form. Write your answers in the blanks.*

1. Look! That is Michel who (crosses, is crossing) the street. *is crossing*
2. Sandra (comes, is coming) to school every day by bus. _____
3. We (was, were) both absent from class yesterday. _____
4. She doesn't (have, has) many friends in the class. _____
5. There aren't (many, much) students in our English class. _____
6. Your book is different (from, as) mine. _____
7. Ms. Tiu is (a, an) very good teacher. _____
8. He is much younger (as, than) Mr. Abbott. _____
9. The weather today is (warmer, more warm) than it was yesterday. _____
10. She speaks English almost (perfect, perfectly). _____
11. He wants (me to go, that I go) with him. _____
12. I didn't hear (someone, anyone) in the room. _____
13. (No, Not) many students attended the meeting. _____
14. He gave (her, to her) the money. _____
15. He told (us, to us) the whole story of his trip. _____
16. It was really (a, an) interesting story. _____
17. Listen! I think it (begins, is beginning) to rain. _____
18. She (does, makes) many mistakes in grammar. _____
19. I don't know how old (is he, he is). _____
20. I can do all of these exercises (easy, easily). _____
21. He often (brings, is bringing) his sister to class. _____
22. (This, These) books belong to the teacher. _____

| Possessive Adjective | Possessive Pronoun | Possessive Adjective | Possessive Pronoun |
|---|---|---|---|
| my | mine | our | ours |
| your | yours | your | yours |
| his | his | their | theirs |
| her | hers | | |
| its | its | | |

| | |
|---|---|
| That is *my* car. | That car is *mine*. |
| Those are *our* seats. | Those seats are *ours*. |

*Write the correct possessive pronouns in the blanks.*

1. This book is *her book.*        *hers*
2. These pencils are *my pencils.* _____
3. This office is *her office.* _____
4. These magazines are *our magazines.* _____
5. These cigarettes are *my cigarettes.* _____
6. Those cigarettes on the table are *your cigarettes.* _____
7. These pencils are *their pencils.* _____
8. I think that this notebook is *your notebook.* _____
9. This newspaper is *my newspaper.* _____
10. This notebook is *her notebook.* _____
11. That hat and coat are *his hat and coat.* _____
12. This umbrella is *my umbrella.* _____
13. These seats are *our seats.* _____
14. That pair of scissors is *her pair of scissors.* _____
15. This classroom is *our classroom.* _____
16. That classroom on the other side of the hall is *your classroom.* _____
17. These books are *Jack and Nina's books.* _____
18. Those books over there on the table are *my books.* _____
19. Is this pen *your pen?* _____
20. No, it is not *my pen;* it is Gregory's. _____
21. Is this pack of cigarettes *your pack of cigarettes?* _____
22. This pack of cigarettes is *his pack of cigarettes.* _____

**Reflexive pronouns refer back to the subject of the sentence when the subject and the object are the same person.**

| The boy hurt *himself.* | We saw *ourselves* in the mirror. |
| She burned *herself.* | |

**Reflexive pronouns are used to emphasize the subject.**

| I *myself* will help you. | The judge *himself* awarded the prize. |

| | |
|---|---|
| myself | ourselves |
| yourself | yourselves |
| himself | themselves |
| herself | |
| itself | |

*Write the correct reflexive pronouns.*

1. Matt shaves _____ every morning.  *himself*
2. Sheila hurt _____ when she fell.  _____
3. I _____ will prepare lunch for everybody.  _____
4. Sam looked at _____ in the mirror.  _____
5. We enjoyed _____ at the party last night.  _____
6. The poor woman shot _____.  _____
7. Be careful! You will cut _____ with that knife.  _____
8. The dog hurt _____ when it jumped over the fence.  _____
9. The child burned _____ on the hot stove.  _____
10. My young son can dress _____ very well.  _____
11. Can your little daughter dress _____ yet?  _____
12. I cut _____ yesterday on a piece of glass.  _____
13. Did you enjoy _____ at John's party last night?  _____
14. The president _____ will deliver the principal address.  _____
15. That horse will hurt _____ if it falls in that hole.  _____
16. We _____ heard Anne shout at the teacher.  _____
17. She says that she _____ will return the book to you.  _____

## 115 Reflexive pronouns 2

**When** by *is placed before the reflexive pronoun, it means "alone, without help."*

I stayed in the house *by myself.* (I stayed in the house without other people.)

She changed the tire *by herself.* (Nobody helped her.)

*For the word* alone, *write the preposition* by *and the correct reflexive pronoun.*

1. She went for a walk in the park *alone.*      *by herself*

2. I don't like to study *alone.* _____

3. He eats lunch every day in the cafeteria *alone.* _____

4. Do you like to eat *alone?* _____

5. The two boys will study *alone.* _____

6. Eva and I will also study *alone.* _____

7. The old woman lives *alone* in a furnished room. _____

8. The dog found its way home *alone.* _____

9. He works *alone* in a small office. _____

10. He often goes for a walk in the park *alone.* _____

11. Do you like to go to the movies *alone?* _____

12. She did all the work *alone.* _____

13. She plans to go to Europe next summer *alone.* _____

14. The boys study *alone* in one group. _____

15. The girls study *alone* in another group. _____

16. I don't want to go to the theater *alone.* _____

17. Some people like to go to the theater *alone,* but I don't. _____

18. They eat *alone* in a special room. _____

19. Beth sat *alone* in a corner all evening long. _____

20. We plan to decorate the apartment *alone.* _____

**Form the present perfect tense with** have **or** has **and the past participle of the main verb.**

> I have stopped.          She has stopped.

**The present perfect tense is used for a past action where the exact time is not mentioned or where there is repeated action in the past. The simple past tense is used to talk about an action that occurred at a definite time in the past. Note these differences.**

| Past | Present Perfect |
|---|---|
| I *went* to Houston last month. | I *have gone* to Houston several times. |
| She *was* there yesterday. | She *has been* there before. |

**All past participles of regular verbs end in** ed **and are the same as in the past tense. The past participles of irregular verbs must be memorized. See the appendix for a list of irregular verbs and their forms.**

*Write the following verbs in the present perfect tense.*

1.  He (spoke) to me about it many times.          *has spoken*
2.  They (finish) their dinner.          _____
3.  I (be) in Washington several times.          _____
4.  I (hear) her sing once or twice.          _____
5.  They (be) good friends for years.          _____
6.  We (learn) many new words.          _____
7.  I (lose) my umbrella.          _____
8.  She (study) that same exercise five or six times.          _____
9.  They (clean) the house from top to bottom.          _____
10.  They (give) up their home in the country.          _____
11.  She (be) late for class many times.          _____
12.  We (drive) to New York from Miami many times.          _____
13.  He (make) and lost several fortunes.          _____
14.  The police (captured) the thief at last.          _____
15.  Ms. Martinez (teach) many students to speak English.          _____
16.  I (see) that same movie three times.          _____
17.  He (lend) me money several times in the past.          _____
18.  I (read) that novel several times.          _____

**The present perfect tense is for an action which began in the past and is still continuing.**

> He has lived there since June. (He is still living there.)
> They have worked here for three years. (They are still working here.)

**Note the difference in meanings in the examples below.**

> I have lived here for two years. (I still live here.)
> I lived there for two years. (But I don't live there anymore.)

*Write the correct tense (past or present perfect) according to the meaning of the sentence.*

1. We are now living on 72nd Street, where we (lived) for almost five years.  *have lived*

2. From 1979 to 1983, we (live) on 96th Street.  _____

3. Joan (study) French in Paris many years ago.  _____

4. Paul is now in the hospital. He (be) there for three weeks. _____

5. World War II (begin) in 1939 and ended in 1945.  _____

6. I am now studying English. I (study) it for almost two years.  _____

7. Marie (study) Spanish when she was in high school.  _____

8. It is natural that George speaks German well because he (speak) it all his life.  _____

9. Gloria (be) our teacher since January.  _____

10. We (be) in California last winter.  _____

11. Mr. and Mrs. Mancini now live in California. They (live) there since 1980.  _____

12. Before she came to the United States, Alice (live) in Venezuela for two years.  _____

13. She (start) to study English as soon as she came to the United States.  _____

14. She (study) English since then.  _____

15. She and I are good friends. In fact, we (be) friends for more than ten years.  _____

16. We (become) friends while we were students.  _____

## negative form

**To form the negative of the present perfect tense, place** not **after** have **or** has. **The contractions** haven't **and** hasn't **are generally used.**

> We have *not (haven't)* been here very long.
>
> It has *not (hasn't)* become very hot yet.

*Change the following sentences from the affirmative to the negative form. Use contractions.*

1. We have been good friends for years.     *haven't been*
2. She has felt well recently.     _____
3. He has worked here for about five years.     _____
4. I have read that story.     _____
5. He has studied English for many years.     _____
6. He has left for Chicago.     _____
7. The lesson has begun.     _____
8. She has been the best student in the class.     _____
9. I have found my pen.     _____
10. I have spoken to him about it.     _____
11. We have known each other a long time.     _____
12. He has been head of that department for two years.     _____
13. She has been a very serious student.     _____
14. Phil has been sick for a long time.     _____
15. They have been in Europe since last January.     _____
16. We have lived in this house for ten years.     _____
17. He has been very kind to her.     _____
18. Nora and Mary have been absent from class all week.     _____
19. You have made this same mistake before.     _____
20. I have had time to do it.     _____
21. I have known him for a long time.     _____
22. He has mentioned it to me.     _____

## question form

**Form questions with the present perfect tense by placing** have **or** has **before the subject.**

> *Have you visited* the Louvre?
> *Has Flight 109* arrived yet?

*Change to the question form. Write the complete verb and subject in the blanks.*

1. He has studied English for many years.      *Has he studied*
2. They have known each other for a long time. _____
3. They have seen that movie. _____
4. He has been in this class since January. _____
5. They have lived there since before the war. _____
6. Helen has been the best student in the class. _____
7. They have finished their dinner. _____
8. The train has left. _____
9. We have learned many new words this week. _____
10. They have been in Europe a long time. _____
11. She has been sick for several weeks. _____
12. They have been in Asia before. _____
13. He has lived in the United States a long time. _____
14. Janet has liked to travel since she was a child. _____
15. They have been friends since their high school days. _____
16. The mail has arrived. _____
17. The school bell has run. _____
18. He has worked as a mechanic. _____
19. They have had their lunch. _____
20. It has been raining all night. _____
21. All the girls have left. _____
22. He has had rather strange dreams. _____

Say **is for direct questions. The exact words of the speaker are used with quotation marks around them.**

> Jan *said,* "When are we leaving?"
>
> She *said* to me, "I will probably arrive late."

Say **is for indirect quotations, also. The words of the speaker are reported.**

> Erica *said* (to me) that she wanted to go to the movies with us.

Tell **is for indirect quotations when the person to whom the words are spoken is mentioned without a preposition.**

> Joseph *told* me that his car was at the mechanic's.

Tell **has some special idiomatic uses.**

| | |
|---|---|
| to tell time | to tell a story |
| to tell a secret | to tell about something |
| to tell the truth | to tell a lie |

**The word** that, **when used as a conjunction to introduce a subordinate clause, as in these sentences, is often dropped in everyday speech. Thus we may say, "He said** that **he was busy" or "He said he was busy." Both forms are used, and both are correct in English.**

*Write the correct form of* say *or* tell *in the blanks.*

1.  The teacher _____ us (that) he was too busy to see us.      *told*
2.  He _____ (that) he had too much work to do.      _____
3.  Peter _____ (that) English was difficult for him.      _____
4.  Can you _____ me where I can find Mr. Smith?      _____
5.  Alice _____ (that) she could not meet us after the lesson.      _____
6.  She _____ (that) she did not feel well.      _____
7.  George _____ me all about his trip to New York.      _____
8.  He _____ (that) he liked New York very much.      _____
9.  You can believe William because he always _____ the truth.      _____
10. Henry _____ yesterday (that) he liked the new teacher very much.      _____

# 121 Review: verb forms

*Write the past tense forms and the past participle forms in the blanks.*

|  | | Past | Past Participle | | | | Past | Past Participle |
|---|---|---|---|---|---|---|---|---|
| 1. | see | saw | seen | 25. | eat | | | |
| 2. | ask | asked | asked | 26. | fall | | | |
| 3. | know | | | 27. | feel | | | |
| 4. | get | | | 28. | study | | | |
| 5. | arrive | | | 29. | live | | | |
| 6. | have | | | 30. | fly | | | |
| 7. | make | | | 31. | forget | | | |
| 8. | find | | | 32. | give | | | |
| 9. | grow | | | 33. | go | | | |
| 10. | leave | | | 34. | hear | | | |
| 11. | walk | | | 35. | be | | | |
| 12. | show | | | 36. | end | | | |
| 13. | say | | | 37. | mean | | | |
| 14. | learn | | | 38. | meet | | | |
| 15. | use | | | 39. | read | | | |
| 16. | tell | | | 40. | ride | | | |
| 17. | bring | | | 41. | ring | | | |
| 18. | wait | | | 42. | run | | | |
| 19. | begin | | | 43. | sell | | | |
| 20. | break | | | 44. | talk | | | |
| 21. | buy | | | 45. | shake | | | |
| 22. | come | | | 46. | sleep | | | |
| 23. | cost | | | 47. | speak | | | |
| 24. | do | | | 48. | take | | | |

121

*Change to the negative form. Write the complete verb in the blanks.*

| | | |
|---|---|---|
| 1. | He speaks English well. | *does not speak* |
| 2. | They went to the movies with us last night. | _____ |
| 3. | They have delivered the mail. | _____ |
| 4. | It is beginning to rain. | _____ |
| 5. | She is a good student. | _____ |
| 6. | She left on the three o'clock train. | _____ |
| 7. | She will return on Wednesday. | _____ |
| 8. | He has many friends in this school. | _____ |
| 9. | He has gone out of town. | _____ |
| 10. | Elaine was at the meeting last night. | _____ |
| 11. | They prepared their homework very well. | _____ |
| 12. | He comes to school by bus. | _____ |
| 13. | There is a magazine on the table. | _____ |
| 14. | Noriko has studied English for a long time. | _____ |
| 15. | She began to study English in elementary school. | _____ |
| 16. | We waited a half hour for him. | _____ |
| 17. | He told us all about it. | _____ |
| 18. | I will be back in an hour. | _____ |
| 19. | I am going to the bookstore to buy some books. | _____ |
| 20. | She has worked in that office since 1983. | _____ |
| 21. | She can speak English perfectly. | _____ |
| 22. | You must tell him about it. | _____ |
| 23. | She writes many letters to her brother. | _____ |
| 24. | He put all his books on the teacher's desk. | _____ |

*Change to the question form. Write the complete verb and subject in the blanks.*

1. He comes to school by bus.     *Does he come*
2. They live on Fifth Avenue.     _____
3. He went to Chicago last week.     _____
4. He will be there at least two weeks.     _____
5. Helen wants to study history next year.     _____
6. She is an excellent student.     _____
7. She is going to study in the United States.     _____
8. Mr. Sanchez lent him the money.     _____
9. You saw him on the bus.     _____
10. His wife was with him.     _____
11. The bus was very crowded at the time.     _____
12. They have a lot of time to study.     _____
13. She wrote you a letter about it.     _____
14. She has studied English for a long time.     _____
15. He has several white shirts.     _____
16. The wind is blowing very hard.     _____
17. She can speak both French and Spanish.     _____
18. They go to the movies together every Saturday.     _____
19. They have seen all the latest movies.     _____
20. He must come back later.     _____
21. She threw the ball.     _____
22. He was here on Wednesday.     _____
23. They sit beside each other in class.     _____
24. She is feeling better today.     _____

*Certain verbs can take both an indirect and direct object. We use the prepositions* to *or* for *if the indirect object comes after the direct object.*

> He gave the money *to* me.
> They bought a present *for* you.
> I told a story *to* everybody.

**When the indirect object comes before the direct object, no preposition is used. Verbs like** give, send, bring, write, tell, lend, pay, **and** buy **follow this pattern.**

> He gave me the money.
> They brought you a present.
> I told everybody a story.

*Restate the following sentences, putting the indirect object before the direct object. Write the verb and the indirect object in the blanks.*

1. He wrote a letter to Susan.                    *wrote Susan*
2. She gave the money to her brother.          _____
3. He sent some post cards to us.                 _____
4. He brought some flowers to her.              _____
5. John wrote a letter to Penny.                  _____
6. The teacher gave some homework to us.   _____
7. He told the story to us.                           _____
8. We sent some flowers to Betty.               _____
9. He brought a box of candy to her.          _____
10. He gave a piece to each of us.               _____
11. I took the flowers to her.                        _____
12. She lent some money to me.                    _____
13. He sold the car to his friend.                  _____
14. He bought a new suit for his son.           _____
15. Please bring the newspaper to me.         _____
16. I gave the tickets to Patricia.                  _____
17. She paid the money to me.                      _____
18. I told the story to Leo.                            _____

## opposites 4

*Write the opposites of the following words.*

| | | | | | |
|---|---|---|---|---|---|
| 1. | clean | *dirty* | 26. | black | _____ |
| 2. | top | _____ | 27. | few | _____ |
| 3. | young | _____ | 28. | sad | _____ |
| 4. | ugly | _____ | 29. | absent | _____ |
| 5. | seldom | _____ | 30. | strong | _____ |
| 6. | buy | _____ | 31. | stop | _____ |
| 7. | awake | _____ | 32. | son | _____ |
| 8. | borrow | _____ | 33. | early | _____ |
| 9. | tight | _____ | 34. | poor | _____ |
| 10. | high | _____ | 35. | far | _____ |
| 11. | laugh | _____ | 36. | careless | _____ |
| 12. | take | _____ | 37. | easy | _____ |
| 13. | outside | _____ | 38. | better | _____ |
| 14. | hard | _____ | 39. | best | _____ |
| 15. | dull | _____ | 40. | dry | _____ |
| 16. | push | _____ | 41. | upstairs | _____ |
| 17. | wide | _____ | 42. | smooth | _____ |
| 18. | empty | _____ | 43. | first | _____ |
| 19. | thick | _____ | 44. | front | _____ |
| 20. | behind | _____ | 45. | same | _____ |
| 21. | expensive | _____ | 46. | north | _____ |
| 22. | woman | _____ | 47. | west | _____ |
| 23. | cry | _____ | 48. | warm | _____ |
| 24. | sweet | _____ | 49. | hot | _____ |
| 25. | rich | _____ | 50. | down | _____ |

# 126 Words used as nouns and verbs

**Many English verbs are also used as nouns with no change in the form of the word. Note the following examples.**

| Verb | Noun |
|---|---|
| They *work* very hard. | Their *work* is difficult. |
| She *loves* seafood. | She has a great *love* for the theater. |
| I *ride* to work on the subway. | I gave Alice a *ride* to work. |

*For additional practice using the same word as different parts of speech, make sentences with the following words:* wish, finish, question, tie, talk, kiss, smile, shout, promise, play, surprise, start, walk, crowd, rest, fall, need, move, sound, notice, ride, turn, *and* watch. *Use each word once as a verb and once as a noun.*

Write noun *if the italicized word of the sentence is used as a noun;* write verb *if the italicized word is used as a verb.*

1. Why do you *look* so sad?  ***verb***
   Everyone noticed the *look* of surprise on his face.  _____ _____

2. We all enjoy the *study* of English.  _____
   They both *study* in the same class.  _____

3. Everyone heard the child's *cries*.  _____
   The baby *cries* all day long.  _____

4. John will *help* us when he comes.  _____
   We all need your *help* badly.  _____

5. Helen wore a very pretty *dress* to the party.  _____
   The baby is still too young to *dress* itself.  _____

6. Both buildings *face* the park.  _____
   The child has a beautiful *face*.  _____

7. After just a few *drinks*, he became drunk.  _____
   John always *drinks* milk with his meals.  _____

8. We *plan* to go to Europe next summer.  _____
   The *plan* to attack England by air failed.  _____

9. All children *love* candy.  _____
   His *love* for her will never die.  _____

# and verb forms

**Note how the following verbs change when they become nouns.**

| Verb | Noun | Verb | Noun |
|------|------|------|------|
| appear | appearance | describe | description |
| explain | explanation | lose | loss |
| arrive | arrival | decide | decision |

*Write the corresponding noun form of these verbs.*

1. to explain — *explanation*
2. to collect — _____
3. to arrive — _____
4. to decide — _____
5. to prove — _____
6. to agree — _____
7. to believe — _____
8. to punish — _____
9. to remain — _____
10. to lose — _____

11. to observe — _____
12. to excite — _____
13. to die — _____
14. to choose — _____
15. to grow — _____
16. to marry — _____
17. to enter — _____
18. to begin — _____
19. to appear — _____
20. to repeat — _____

*Write the corresponding verb form of these nouns.*

21. description — *describe*
22. explanation — _____
23. satisfaction — _____
24. laughter — _____
25. growth — _____
26. existence — _____
27. proof — _____
28. agreement — _____
29. arrival — _____
30. location — _____

31. appearance — _____
32. arrangement — _____
33. protection — _____
34. discovery — _____
35. explosion — _____
36. imagination — _____
37. loss — _____
38. failure — _____
39. entrance — _____
40. beginning — _____

*Select the correct answer and write it in the space provided.*

1. The opposite of to *put on* is to (put away, take off, pick up, call on).  *take off*

2. The opposite of to *turn on* is to (turn down, turn off, put away, wait on).  _____

3. To *get on* the bus is to (leave it, enter it, wait for it, signal to it).  _____

4. I'd *rather study* means that I (like to study, study hard, prefer to study).  _____

5. *Right away* means (much later, immediately, correct, wrong).  _____

6. To *call up* someone is to (criticize, meet, like, telephone) him or her.  _____

7. To *call on* someone is to (write to, visit, wait for, telephone) him or her.  _____

8. To *get off* the bus is to (enter it, leave it, pay one's fare).  _____

9. If I *take off* my coat, it means that I (put it on, remove it, hang it up, put it away).  _____

10. The opposite of to *stand up* is to (leave, wait, sit down, arrive).  _____

11. *At last* means (first, soon, finally, seldom).  _____

12. If I am *tired out*, I am (rather tired, extremely tired, a little tired).  _____

13. *Right here* means (near here, exactly here, over there).  _____

14. To *look for* something is to (lose it, try to find it, need it, forget it).  _____

15. If something is *all right*, it means that it is (out of order, satisfactory, ready, necessary).  _____

16. *Little by little* means (soon, gradually, rapidly, never.)  _____

17. To *find out* about something is to (remember, get information about, discuss) it.  _____

18. *Look out!* means (look out the window, wait, be careful).  _____

# Answer Key

Exercise 1

| | | | | |
|---|---|---|---|---|
| 2. is | 5. are | 8. I'm | 11. She's | 14. are |
| 3. is | 6. He's | 9. We're | 12. is | 15. They're |
| 4. are | 7. You're | 10. is | 13. It's | |

Exercise 2

| | | | | |
|---|---|---|---|---|
| 2. are | 7. am | 11. are | 15. is | 19. is |
| 3. is | 8. is | 12. is | 16. are | 20. is |
| 4. is | 9. are | 13. is | 17. are | 21. are |
| 5. are | 10. are | 14. is | 18. am | 22. are |
| 6. are | | | | |

Exercise 3

| | | | |
|---|---|---|---|
| 2. isn't | 7. aren't | 12. isn't | 17. aren't |
| 3. aren't | 8. isn't | 13. aren't | 18. isn't |
| 4. am not | 9. aren't | 14. aren't | 19. aren't |
| 5. isn't | 10. aren't | 15. aren't | 20. aren't |
| 6. isn't | 11. aren't | 16. aren't | 21. aren't |

Exercise 4

| | | |
|---|---|---|
| 2. Is he | 9. Are they | 16. Are Joe and he |
| 3. Is today | 10. Are Henry and she | 17. Are you and |
| 4. Are Antonia and he | 11. Are we | 18. Are they |
| 5. Are you and George | 12. Are Mr. and Mrs. Jones | 19. Is the teacher |
| 6. Are she and Mary | 13. Is this | 20. Is this |
| 7. Are the windows | 14. Is this lesson | 21. Are they |
| 8. Is the door | 15. Is she | 22. Is he |

Exercise 5

| | | | |
|---|---|---|---|
| 2. have | 7. have | 12. have | 17. have |
| 3. have | 8. has | 13. has | 18. has |
| 4. have | 9. has | 14. has | 19. have |
| 5. has | 10. have | 15. has | 20. have |
| 6. has | 11. have | 16. have | 21. has |

Exercise 6

| | | | |
|---|---|---|---|
| 2. don't have | 7. don't have | 12. don't have | 17. doesn't have |
| 3. doesn't have | 8. doesn't have | 13. doesn't have | 18. doesn't have |
| 4. doesn't have | 9. doesn't have | 14. doesn't have | 19. don't have |
| 5. doesn't have | 10. don't have | 15. don't have | 20. don't have |
| 6. doesn't have | 11. doesn't have | 16. doesn't have | |

2. Does this room have
3. Does that girl have
4. Do you have
5. Does Helen have
6. Does the cat have
7. Do these dogs have
8. Does Mary have
9. Do you have
10. Does Mr. Shapiro have
11. Does John have
12. Do we have
13. Does this book have
14. Does Mr. Smith have
15. Do you have
16. Do most watches have
17. Does every student have
18. Do we have
19. Does Helen have
20. Does Miss Pappas have

2. write
3. walk
4. walks
5. sit
6. sits
7. write
8. opens
9. works
10. smokes
11. come
12. comes
13. walk
14. read
15. eat
16. eats
17. play
18. plays
19. play
20. works
21. wants

2. studies
3. goes
4. go
5. carries
6. carries
7. plays
8. plays
9. play
10. play
11. does
12. does
13. try
14. try
15. tries
16. want
17. wants
18. go
19. teaches
20. watches

3. He/She lives
4. He/She is
5. He/She wants
6. He/She teaches
7. He/She is
8. He/She goes
9. He/She does
10. He/She sees
11. He/She is
12. He/She carries
13. He/She has
14. He/She studies
15. He/She plays
16. He/She tries
17. He/She eats
18. He/She tries
19. He/She studies
20. He/She passes
21. He/She goes
22. He/She has

3. classes
4. brothers
5. friends
6. cousins
7. watches
8. cafeterias
9. doors
10. windows
11. wishes
12. teachers
13. pencils
14. pens
15. notebooks
16. matches
17. tails
18. eyes
19. noses
20. dresses
21. women
22. lunches
23. students
24. sisters
25. hats
26. men
27. coats
28. teeth

2. The men speak
3. The boys play
4. The children play
5. The mice run
6. The cats run
7. They speak
8. We play
9. They go
10. The buses arrive
11. The classes begin
12. The women are
13. The dishes are
14. The dresses are
15. The pencils are
16. The trains leave
17. The watches run
18. The boxes are
19. The churches are
20. The classes end
21. The buses are
22. The children are
23. The women are
24. The men are

## Exercise 13

| | | | | |
|---|---|---|---|---|
| 2. her | 6. her | 10. his | 14. its | 18. your |
| 3. my | 7. our | 11. his | 15. my | 19. her |
| 4. our | 8. their | 12. my | 16. our | |
| 5. my | 9. their | 13. its | 17. their | |

## Exercise 14

| | | | |
|---|---|---|---|
| 2. are | 8. is | 14. is | 20. are |
| 3. are | 9. are | 15. are | 21. is |
| 4. are | 10. are | 16. are | 22. is |
| 5. is | 11. are | 17. are | |
| 6. are | 12. is | 18. is | |
| 7. are | 13. are | 19. is | |

## Exercise 15

| | | | |
|---|---|---|---|
| 2. isn't | 8. aren't | 14. isn't | 20. isn't |
| 3. isn't | 9. isn't | 15. aren't | 21. aren't |
| 4. aren't | 10. aren't | 16. aren't | 22. isn't |
| 5. aren't | 11. aren't | 17. isn't | |
| 6. aren't | 12. isn't | 18. isn't | |
| 7. isn't | 13. aren't | 19. aren't | |

## Exercise 16

| | | | |
|---|---|---|---|
| 2. Are there | 8. Is there | 14. Are there | 20. Are there |
| 3. Is there | 9. Is there | 15. Are there | 21. Is there |
| 4. Is there | 10. Are there | 16. Is there | 22. Are there |
| 5. Is there | 11. Is there | 17. Is there | |
| 6. Are there | 12. Are there | 18. Are there | |
| 7. Are there | 13. Is there | 19. Are there | |

## Exercise 17

| | | | | | |
|---|---|---|---|---|---|
| 3. a | 11. an | 19. a | 27. an | 35. a | 43. an |
| 4. a | 12. an | 20. a | 28. an | 36. a | 44. a |
| 5. an | 13. an | 21. an | 29. an | 37. an | |
| 6. a | 14. a | 22. an | 30. a | 38. a | |
| 7. an | 15. an | 23. an | 31. a | 39. an | |
| 8. a | 16. an | 24. a | 32. an | 40. a | |
| 9. an | 17. a | 25. an | 33. an | 41. an | |
| 10. a | 18. an | 26. a | 34. an | 42. a | |

## Exercise 18

3. Those men in the office are
4. These apples are
5. These exercises are
6. Those pocketbooks on the table belong
7. These lessons are
8. These are
9. Those automobiles belong
10. Those are

11. Those windows over there are
12. Those are
13. These letters are
14. Those letters are
15. Those houses near the corner are
16. These umbrellas belong
17. These exercises are
18. These are
19. Those are
20. Those hats belong

2. These
3. are
4. has
5. don't have
6. speaks
7. come
8. churches
9. leaves
10. Tomatoes
11. Does
12. its
13. are
14. isn't
15. an
16. an
17. an
18. Those
19. teaches
20. tries
21. are
22. have
23. is
24. a
25. an

2. Don't come
3. Don't sit
4. Don't open
5. Don't close
6. Don't ask
7. Don't take
8. Don't wait
9. Don't put
10. Don't hang
11. Don't study
12. Don't write
13. Don't help
14. Don't speak
15. Don't use
16. Don't give
17. Don't sit
18. Don't drive
19. Don't tell
20. Don't look

2. me
3. her
4. them
5. her
6. him
7. us
8. them
9. them
10. me
11. him
12. her
13. us
14. her
15. me
16. him
17. them
18. us
19. me
20. them
21. us

2. her
3. them
4. us
5. them
6. her
7. them
8. her
9. him
10. him
11. her
12. you
13. her
14. him
15. them
16. them
17. you
18. them
19. them
20. her
21. them

2. February
3. March
4. December
5. July
6. October
7. April
8. July
9. November
10. hot
11. cold
12. Sunday
13. Monday
14. Saturday
15. Tuesday
16. Friday
17. Tuesday

2. was
3. was
4. were
5. were
6. was
7. were
8. was
9. was
10. were
11. was
12. was
13. was
14. were
15. was
16. were
17. were
18. were
19. was
20. were
21. was

2. arrived
3. ended
4. lived
5. studied
6. finished
7. liked
8. answered
9. walked
10. following
11. needed
12. waited
13. wanted
14. learned
15. used
16. listened
17. watched

3. 2
4. 2
5. 2
6. 1
7. 2
8. 1
9. 1
10. 2
11. 2
12. 1
13. 1
14. 1
15. 1
16. 2
17. 2
18. 1
19. 1
20. 1
21. 2
22. 1
23. 2
24. 1
25. 1
26. 1
27. 2
28. 1
29. 1
30. 2
31. 1
32. 1
33. 2
34. 1
35. 1
36. 1
37. 2
38. 1
39. 1
40. 1

2. bought
3. read
4. drank
5. had
6. sat
7. ate
8. got up
9. spoke
10. put
11. came
12. had
13. drank
14. sat
15. spoke
16. got up
17. ate
18. spun
19. bought
20. wrote

2. December
3. November
4. before
5. after
6. seven
7. Sunday
8. Saturday
9. before
10. after
11. twenty-eight
12. winter
13. March
14. June
15. sat
16. bought
17. children
18. women
19. sixty
20. sixty
21. short

2. low
3. out
4. bad
5. no
6. absent
7. down
8. white
9. few
10. after
11. difficult
12. pull
13. cold
14. last
15. little/small
16. expensive
17. sour
18. late
19. cool
20. hard
21. night
22. buy
23. thin
24. good
25. take
26. up
27. awake
28. in
29. yes
30. false
31. present
32. black
33. many
34. before
35. easy
36. push
37. hot
38. warm
39. stand
40. first
41. big
42. cheap
43. sweet
44. day
45. start/begin
46. sell

2. in
3. before
4. at
5. to
6. in
7. by
8. of
9. at
10. in
11. of
12. for
13. in
14. on
15. to
16. after
17. to
18. in
19. at
20. by
21. in
22. on
23. for
24. in

| | | | |
|---|---|---|---|
| 2. was | 7. isn't | 12. us | 17. do | 22. are |
| 3. speaks | 8. an | 13. were | 18. Were | 23. an |
| 4. got | 9. put | 14. watched | 19. a | 24. ate |
| 5. them | 10. was | 15. from | 20. an | |
| 6. her | 11. Does | 16. study | 21. gets | |

| | | | |
|---|---|---|---|
| 2. was | 7. were | 12. read | 17. ended |
| 3. drank | 8. had | 13. bought | 18. was |
| 4. came | 9. had | 14. smoked | 19. were |
| 5. needed | 10. spoke | 15. learned | 20. was |
| 6. talked | 11. were | 16. asked | 21. followed |

| | | | |
|---|---|---|---|
| 2. have | 7. are | 12. writes | 17. likes |
| 3. buy | 8. is | 13. puts | 18. wants |
| 4. speak | 9. wait | 14. needs | 19. is |
| 5. reads | 10. asks | 15. stops | 20. are |
| 6. eat | 11. get | 16. are | 21. come |

| | | |
|---|---|---|
| 2. should not speak | 9. cannot play | 16. should not sit |
| 3. may not smoke | 10. may not open | 17. must not tell |
| 4. may not be | 11. may not be | 18. cannot go |
| 5. must not see | 12. cannot do | 19. may not sit |
| 6. cannot telephone | 13. may not go | 20. must not do |
| 7. should not tell | 14. may not wait | |
| 8. must not go | 15. cannot meet | |

| | | |
|---|---|---|
| 2. Should he wait | 9. Must we explain | 16. Can she attend |
| 3. May they smoke | 10. May Toby wait | 17. Can he play |
| 4. Can Sam meet | 11. May they sit | 18. Can they speak |
| 5. Must he go | 12. Should you stay | 19. Can Ricardo understand |
| 6. Should she tell | 13. Can he meet | 20. Can she do |
| 7. Can she go | 14. Can he swim | |
| 8. May he wait | 15. Must you write | |

| | | | |
|---|---|---|---|
| 2. do not go | don't go | 7. does not begin | doesn't begin |
| 3. does not come | doesn't come | 8. does not end | doesn't end |
| 4. do not know | don't know | 9. do not stop | don't stop |
| 5. does not rain | doesn't rain | 10. do not write | don't write |
| 6. does not run | doesn't run | 11. does not speak | doesn't speak |

| 12. do not walk | don't walk | 17. do not arrive | don't arrive |
| 13. do not like | don't like | 18. do not need | don't need |
| 14. does not live | doesn't live | 19. do not understand | don't understand |
| 15. does not work | doesn't work | 20. does not get up | doesn't get up |
| 16. do not go | don't go | | |

Exercise 37

2. Do they speak
3. Does he get up
4. Do the Browns eat
5. Do they like
6. Does he want
7. Do the students prefer
8. Does he talk
9. Do they live
10. Does he take
11. Does John smoke
12. Does she dance
13. Do they know
14. Do you understand
15. Do they get up
16. Does he read
17. Do we want
18. Do they come
19. Does Mary arrive
20. Does it rain
21. Does he eat
22. Do they sell

Exercise 38

2. do
3. does
4. do
5. does
6. does
7. do
8. do
9. does
10. does
11. do
12. does
13. do
14. does
15. does
16. do
17. do
18. does
19. do
20. do
21. does
22. do

Exercise 39

2. weren't
3. wasn't
4. wasn't
5. weren't
6. weren't
7. wasn't
8. weren't
9. weren't
10. weren't
11. wasn't
12. wasn't
13. wasn't
14. weren't
15. wasn't
16. wasn't
17. weren't
18. wasn't
19. wasn't
20. weren't
21. wasn't
22. weren't

Exercise 40

2. Were they
3. Was he
4. Were there
5. Were the windows
6. Was the door
7. Were they
8. Was there
9. Were we
10. Are they
11. Were we
12. Was the lesson
13. Was the teacher
14. Were he and she
15. Were the exercises
16. Was the woman
17. Was there
18. Was it
19. Were there
20. Was there
21. Was Angela
22. Were you

Exercise 41

2. She didn't come
3. We didn't eat
4. I didn't buy
5. The child didn't drink
6. She didn't want
7. He didn't need
8. I didn't wait
9. He didn't read
10. We didn't watch
11. He didn't have
12. He didn't like
13. She didn't put
14. I didn't get up
15. John didn't come
16. He didn't ask
17. We didn't learn
18. I didn't write
19. The bus didn't stop
20. We didn't eat
21. She didn't sit
22. She didn't get

2. Did she wait
3. Did they write
4. Did the bus stop
5. Did they have
6. Did she want
7. Did he prefer
8. Did Monica know
9. Did you get up
10. Did they come
11. Did Julio read
12. Did they live
13. Did she speak
14. Did we talk
15. Did he buy
16. Did she put on
17. Did it rain
18. Did he arrive
19. Did she write
20. Did we eat
21. Did they sit
22. Did the lesson end

2. in
3. at
4. in
5. for
6. at
7. for
8. on
9. about
10. in front of
11. above
12. before
13. after
14. of
15. on
16. for
17. from
18. on
19. by
20. with
21. for
22. about
23. in
24. over

2. heard
3. felt
4. rode
5. saw
6. told
7. began
8. knew
9. left
10. cost
11. gave
12. sold
13. stood
14. understood
15. saw
16. fell
17. left
18. began
19. went
20. told
21. rode
22. sold

2. felt
3. post office
4. home
5. November
6. take off
7. walked
8. ears
9. fare
10. gloves
11. pull
12. cold
13. sneeze
14. expensive
15. w
16. 1
17. breakfast

2. gets
3. These
4. see
5. did
6. an
7. a
8. an
9. did you go
10. to speak
11. have
12. are
13. were
14. ate
15. got
16. are
17. go
18. her
19. speak
20. them
21. do
22. weren't
23. Did
24. came

3. didn't have
4. didn't have
5. didn't have
6. didn't have
7. had
8. didn't have
9. didn't have
10. didn't have
11. had
12. didn't have
13. didn't have
14. had
15. didn't have
16. had
17. didn't have
18. didn't have
19. didn't have
20. didn't have
21. had
22. didn't have

## Exercise 48

2. Did they have
3. Did you have
4. Did she have
5. Did the teacher have
6. Did you have
7. Did we have
8. Did she have
9. Did they have
10. Did they have
11. Did she have
12. Did your father have
13. Did Helen have
14. Did he have
15. Did he have
16. Did this room have
17. Did the movie have
18. Did the child have
19. Did we have
20. Did he have

## Exercise 49

3. s
4. z
5. z
6. z
7. s
8. z
9. z
10. s
11. s
12. z
13. z
14. s
15. z
16. s
17. s
18. z
19. z
20. s
21. s
22. z
23. z
24. z
25. s
26. z
27. z
28. z
29. s
30. z
31. z
32. s
33. z
34. s
35. z
36. s
37. z
38. z
39. s
40. z
41. z
42. z
43. s
44. z

## Exercise 50

3. in
4. smooth
5. wet
6. true
7. first
8. after
9. wife
10. take
11. rich
12. boy
13. brother
14. hard
15. present
16. man
17. dry
18. polite
19. husband
20. son
21. white
22. dull
23. single
24. happy
25. little/small
26. bad
27. dangerous
28. clean
29. light
30. early
31. full
32. winter
33. slow
34. west
35. south
36. difficult
37. stand
38. sweet
39. old
40. absent
41. sharp
42. empty
43. sit
44. push
45. sell
46. far
47. tight
48. outside

## Exercise 51

2. He
3. They
4. her
5. him
6. them
7. It
8. They
9. her
10. it
11. them
12. it
13. We
14. you
15. She
16. him
17. It
18. it
19. They
20. them
21. us
22. We
23. He
24. him

## Exercise 52

2. dishes
3. children
4. cities
5. books
6. knives
7. boxes
8. potatoes
9. classes
10. buses
11. streets
12. exercises
13. wishes
14. copies
15. pens
16. keys
17. churches
18. heroes
19. women
20. pianos
21. halves
22. brothers
23. leaves
24. dresses
25. sisters
26. matches
27. letters
28. hats
29. men
30. lunches
31. feet
32. roofs
33. echoes
34. ladies
35. mice
36. wives
37. boys
38. monkeys
39. kisses
40. faces
41. dogs
42. watches
43. teeth
44. windows

2. will work
3. will speak
4. will come
5. will walk

6. will bring
7. will open
8. will study
9. will bring

10. will play
11. will carry
12. will speak
13. will write

14. will bring
15. will arrive
16. will have
17. will eat

18. will leave
19. will like
20. will teach

2. They'll be
3. She'll be
4. He'll be
5. It'll be

6. I'll be
7. You'll be
8. He'll be
9. It'll be

10. We'll be
11. You'll be
12. There'll be
13. She'll be

14. They'll be
15. It'll be
16. He'll be
17. I'll be

18. She'll be
19. We'll be
20. They'll be

2. won't be
3. won't be
4. won't arrive
5. won't meet
6. won't bring

7. won't wait
8. won't return
9. won't help
10. won't leave
11. won't sign

12. won't eat
13. won't be
14. won't see
15. won't write
16. won't be

17. won't tell
18. won't be
19. won't like
20. won't be

2. Will she write
3. Will they leave
4. Will he be
5. Will he study
6. Will we have
7. Will he pay

8. Will they make
9. Will Rita be
10. Will we write
11. Will they wait
12. Will the lesson begin
13. Will it end

14. Will the meeting last
15. Will she speak
16. Will they be
17. Will they travel
18. Will there be
19. Will you have

2. a. are
   b. were
   c. will be
3. a. is
   b. was
   c. will be

4. a. are
   b. were
   c. will be
5. a. are
   b. were
   c. will be

6. a. are
   b. were
   c. will be
7. a. is
   b. was
   c. will

8. a. are
   b. were
   c. will be
9. a. am
   b. was
   c. will be

2. a. aren't
   b. weren't
   c. won't be
3. a. aren't
   b. weren't
   c. won't be

4. a. aren't
   b. weren't
   c. won't be
5. a. isn't
   b. wasn't
   c. won't be

6. a. aren't
   b. weren't
   c. won't be
7. a. aren't
   b. weren't
   c. won't be

8. a. isn't
   b. wasn't
   c. won't be

2.  a. Is the door
    b. Was the door
    c. Will the door be
3.  a. Is it
    b. Was it
    c. Will it be
4.  a. Are they
    b. Were they
    c. Will they be

5.  a. Are there
    b. Were there
    c. Will there be
6.  a. Is Felipe
    b. Was Felipe
    c. Will Felipe be
7.  a. Are the exercises
    b. Were the exercises
    c. Will the exercises be

8.  a. Are we
    b. Were we
    c. Will we be
9.  a. Is the train
    b. Was the train
    c. Will the train be

2.  a. eat
    b. ate
    c. will eat
3.  a. have
    b. had
    c. will have

4.  a. arrive
    b. arrived
    c. will arrive
5.  a. takes
    b. took
    c. will take

6.  a. goes
    b. went
    c. will go
7.  a. waits
    b. waited
    c. will wait

8.  a. ends
    b. ended
    c. will end
9.  a. get
    b. got
    c. will get

2.  a. don't live
    b. didn't live
    c. won't live
3.  a. doesn't come
    b. didn't come
    c. won't come

4.  a. don't have
    b. didn't have
    c. won't have
5.  a. don't go
    b. didn't go
    c. won't go

6.  a. doesn't begin
    b. didn't begin
    c. won't begin
7.  a. don't read
    b. didn't read
    c. won't read

8.  a. don't get up
    b. didn't get up
    c. won't get up

2.  a. Does the train leave
    b. Did the train leave
    c. Will the train leave
3.  a. Does our lesson end
    b. Did our lesson end
    c. Will our lesson end
4.  a. Do we eat
    b. Did we eat
    c. Will we eat

5.  a. Does the bus stop
    b. Did the bus stop
    c. Will the bus stop
6.  a. Does Peter get up
    b. Did Peter get up
    c. Will Peter get up
7.  a. Does she write
    b. Did she write
    c. Will she write

8.  a. Does John go
    b. Did John go
    c. Will John go
9.  a. Do they wake up
    b. Did they wake up
    c. Will they wake up

3. soft
4. softly
5. cleverly
6. clever

7. carefully
8. careful
9. slowly
10. slow

11. quickly
12. quick
13. easy
14. easily

15. frequently
16. frequent
17. serious

| | | | | | |
|---|---|---|---|---|---|
| 3. well | 7. well | 10. well | 13. good | 16. good | 19. well |
| 4. good | 8. well | 11. well | 14. well | 17. well | 20. well |
| 5. good | 9. good | 12. well | 15. well | 18. good | 21. good |
| 6. well | | | | | |

| | | | | | |
|---|---|---|---|---|---|
| 3. many | 10. much | 17. many | 24. much | 31. much | 38. much |
| 4. much | 11. many | 18. much | 25. many | 32. many | 39. many |
| 5. many | 12. many | 19. much | 26. much | 33. much | 40. much |
| 6. many | 13. much | 20. much | 27. much | 34. much | 41. much |
| 7. much | 14. much | 21. many | 28. many | 35. many | 42. much |
| 8. much | 15. many | 22. much | 29. many | 36. many | 43. many |
| 9. many | 16. much | 23. much | 30. much | 37. many | 44. much |

| | | | | | |
|---|---|---|---|---|---|
| 2. not | 5. not | 8. No | 11. not | 14. no | 17. not |
| 3. no | 6. Not | 9. not | 12. no | 15. no | 18. not |
| 4. not | 7. no | 10. no | 13. not | 16. not | |

| | | | |
|---|---|---|---|
| 2. took | 8. became | 14. thought | 20. made |
| 3. brought | 9. made | 15. became | 21. broke |
| 4. forgot | 10. found | 16. took | 22. sang |
| 5. taught | 11. shook | 17. caught | |
| 6. lost | 12. caught | 18. forgot | |
| 7. rang | 13. fought | 19. rang | |

| | | | | |
|---|---|---|---|---|
| 2. into | 7. above/over | 12. until | 17. in | 22. for |
| 3. for | 8. on | 13. to | 18. behind | 23. for |
| 4. into | 9. over | 14. to | 19. near | 24. at |
| 5. for | 10. for | 15. from | 20. about | |
| 6. by | 11. for | 16. along | 21. at | |

| | | |
|---|---|---|
| 2. Washington, D.C. | 10. before | 18. will |
| 3. Alaska | 11. after | 19. ears |
| 4. Rhode Island | 12. cheap | 20. sour |
| 5. fourteen | 13. west | 21. put on |
| 6. six | 14. sixty | 22. now |
| 7. forty | 15. saw | 23. drink |
| 8. December | 16. sat | 24. one syllable |
| 9. June | 17. these | |

## Exercise 70

| | | | |
|---|---|---|---|
| 2. December | 6. k | 10. some | 14. recently |
| 3. November | 7. asked | 11. the first | 15. could |
| 4. pear | 8. mile | 12. find | 16. menu |
| 5. w | 9. sneeze | 13. lost | 17. umbrella |

## Exercise 71

| | | | | |
|---|---|---|---|---|
| 2. came | 7. can speak | 12. Not | 17. Tomatoes | 22. Does |
| 3. did | 8. has | 13. caught | 18. leaves | 23. Do |
| 4. an | 9. us | 14. well | 19. them | 24. Do |
| 5. were | 10. Does | 15. beautifully | 20. on | 25. an |
| 6. much | 11. Not | 16. carefully | 21. Was | |

## Exercise 72

| | | | |
|---|---|---|---|
| 2. is waiting | 7. are making | 12. is knocking | 17. are laughing |
| 3. is beginning | 8. is ringing | 13. is walking | 18. is stopping |
| 4. are beginning | 9. are studying | 14. is reading | 19. are building |
| 5. are taking | 10. is leaving | 15. is blowing | |
| 6. am beginning | 11. is looking | 16. is looking | |

## Exercise 73

| | | | |
|---|---|---|---|
| 3. does | 8. writes | 13. is having | 18. is getting |
| 4. is beginning | 9. is writing | 14. have | 19. gets |
| 5. is blowing | 10. is waving | 15. are having | 20. are buying |
| 6. smokes | 11. is walking | 16. stops | |
| 7. is smoking | 12. have | 17. is stopping | |

## Exercise 74

| | | | |
|---|---|---|---|
| 2. is going | 8. is stopping | 14. is wearing | 20. is speaking |
| 3. are coming | 9. is driving | 15. is waiting | 21. is teaching |
| 4. is blowing | 10. is leaving | 16. are learning | 22. is putting |
| 5. are falling | 11. is helping | 17. is preparing | |
| 6. is correcting | 12. is eating | 18. is wearing | |
| 7. is preparing | 13. is doing | 19. is playing | |

## Exercise 75

| | | |
|---|---|---|
| 2. isn't ringing | 9. isn't having | 16. aren't speaking |
| 3. aren't changing | 10. isn't reading | 17. isn't blowing |
| 4. aren't making | 11. aren't watching | 18. isn't getting |
| 5. I'm not learning | 12. isn't doing | 19. I'm not getting |
| 6. aren't selling | 13. aren't traveling | 20. isn't turning |
| 7. isn't stopping | 14. isn't laughing | 21. isn't showing |
| 8. I'm not having | 15. isn't looking | 22. isn't taking |

2. Is she waiting
3. Is the telephone ringing
4. Are the police investigating
5. Is the mail carrier delivering
6. Are the birds flying
7. Are they taking
8. Is Adam reading
9. Is Roy preparing
10. Are they taking
11. Is the sky getting
12. Is the wind beginning
13. Is William becoming
14. Is her cousin studying
15. Are they discussing
16. Is Sara's family moving
17. Is the bus stopping
18. Is she getting
19. Is he signing
20. Are they shaking
21. Is Annette being
22. Is Mr. Berger taking

2. is going to meet — He's going to meet
3. is going to buy — She's going to buy
4. are going to go — We're going to go
5. are going to build — They're going to build
6. is going to take — He's going to take
7. are going to have — We're going to have
8. is going to rain — it's going to rain
9. am going to have — I'm going to have
10. is going to meet — She's going to meet
11. are going to watch — We're going to watch
12. is going to study — He's going to study
13. is going to be — she's going to be

2. Yes, I will. — No, I won't.
3. Yes, she will. — No, she won't.
4. Yes, it is. — No, it isn't.
5. Yes, it is. — No, it isn't.
6. Yes, there are. — No, there aren't.
7. Yes, we did. — No, we didn't.
8. Yes, I do. — No, I didn't.
9. Yes, I am. — No, I'm not.
10. Yes, he is. — No, he isn't.
11. Yes, they are. — No, they aren't.
12. Yes, it is. — No, it isn't.
13. Yes, we are. — No, we aren't.
14. Yes, I can. — No, I can't.
15. Yes, it did. — No, it didn't.

2. _____
3. The
4. _____
5. The
6. _____
7. The
8. _____
9. the
10. _____
11. The
12. _____
13. The

| | | | |
|---|---|---|---|
| 2. drove | 7. did | 12. kept | 17. blew |
| 3. blew | 8. stole | 13. slept | 18. cut |
| 4. slept | 9. meant | 14. did | 19. stole |
| 5. hit | 10. cut | 15. met | 20. hit |
| 6. swept | 11. shut | 16. drove | 21. kept |

| | | | | |
|---|---|---|---|---|
| 2. which | 5. which | 8. who | 11. which | 14. who |
| 3. which | 6. which | 9. which | 12. which | 15. which |
| 4. who | 7. who | 10. who | 13. which | 16. who |

| | |
|---|---|
| 2. more interesting than | 8. more tired than |
| 3. sweeter than | 9. larger than |
| 4. warmer than | 10. longer than |
| 5. easier than | 11. busier than |
| 6. more intelligent than | 12. worse than |
| 7. colder than | 13. shallower than |

| | | |
|---|---|---|
| 2. sooner than | 7. later than | 12. more lazily than |
| 3. more loudly than | 8. faster than | 13. better than |
| 4. more quickly than | 9. more slowly than | 14. more easily than |
| 5 better than | 10. more carefully than | 15. sooner than |
| 6. more beautifully than | 11. harder than | 16. more often than |

| | | |
|---|---|---|
| 2. the most athletic | 7. the hottest | 12. the best |
| 3. the largest | 8. the most difficult | 13. the largest |
| 4. the most intelligent | 9. the widest | 14. the worst |
| 5. the best | 10. the busiest | 15. the coldest |
| 6. the longest | 11. the friendliest | |

| | | | |
|---|---|---|---|
| 2. east | 8. longer | 14. south | 20. eyes |
| 3. expensive | 9. twenty-six | 15. one syllable | 21. winter |
| 4. k | 10. best | 16. two syllables | 22. Civil War |
| 5. could | 11. George Washington | 17. third | |
| 6. spoke | 12. three | 18. fourth | |
| 7. sixty | 13. centimeter | 19. telephone | |

2. needed
3. took
4. taught
5. told
6. thought
7. heard
8. wrote
9. counted
10. had
11. prepared
12. worked
13. swept
14. stole

15. stood
16. slept
17. painted
18. pushed
19. pulled
20. wept
21. sat
22. sang
23. came
24. shut
25. shook
26. sold
27. saw

28. rang
29. rode
30. read
31. put
32. visited
33. studied
34. lived
35. met
36. meant
37. made
38. lost
39. left
40. knew

41. kept
42. been
43. liked
44. hit
45. wanted
46. gave
47. got
48. forgot
49. found
50. fought
51. felt
52. ate
53. drove

54. drank
55. did
56. cut
57. cost
58. caught
59. bought
60. sprang
61. broke
62. blew
63. began
64. became
65. started
66. stopped

2. feel
3. got
4. know
5. hit

6. wrong, left
7. immediately
8. choose
9. is

10. spring
11. hear
12. the third
13. soft

14. will
15. walked
16. wanted

2. for
3. on
4. for
5. at
6. At

7. from
8. about
9. at
10. about
11. for

12. for
13. on
14. to
15. by
16. on

17. over
18. behind
19. to
20. for
21. out

22. for
23. across
24. under
25. between

2. Those
3. either
4. could
5. them
6. Not

7. than
8. belongs
9. speak
10. well
11. beautifully

12. an
13. an
14. a
15. much
16. Were

17. who
18. were
19. carefully
20. well
21. to go

22. to learn
23. did
24. speak

2. some
3. any
4. some
5. some

6. any
7. any
8. some
9. some

10. any
11. some
12. any
13. some

14. any
15. some
16. any
17. some

18. any
19. some
20. any
21. some

2. something
3. something
4. anything
5. somewhere
6. anywhere

7. someone
8. anyone
9. someone
10. anyone
11. someone

12. something
13. anything
14. somewhere
15. anywhere
16. something

17. anything
18. something
19. somebody
20. anybody
21. anybody

| | | | |
|---|---|---|---|
| 2. old | 12. sharp | 22. cheap | 32. forget | 42. hard |
| 3. sell | 13. sad | 23. bring | 33. rough | 43. winter |
| 4. seldom | 14. pull | 24. thick | 34. high | 44. early |
| 5. ugly | 15. narrow | 25. short | 35. behind | 45. light |
| 6. tight | 16. careless | 26. many | 36. hot | 46. up |
| 7. low | 17. full | 27. dirty | 37. low | 47. stand |
| 8. cry | 18. black | 28. present | 38. summer | 48. little/small |
| 9. safe | 19. thin | 29. push | 39. bad | |
| 10. outside | 20. start/begin | 30. difficult | 40. west | |
| 11. soft | 21. in front of | 31. wide | 41. sweet | |

| | | | | | |
|---|---|---|---|---|---|
| 2. t | 9. b | 16. b | 23. l | 30. g | 37. h |
| 3. k | 10. l | 17. g | 24. l | 31. w | 38. w |
| 4. k | 11. k | 18. b | 25. k | 32. k | 39. c |
| 5. t | 12. l | 19. b | 26. d | 33. s | 40. p |
| 6. h | 13. t | 20. b | 27. w | 34. b | 41. k |
| 7. w | 14. s | 21. h | 28. l | 35. c | 42. g |
| 8. t | 15. w | 22. k | 29. w | 36. c | |

| | | | | |
|---|---|---|---|---|
| 2. lent | 6. shot | 10. said | 14. won | 18. flew |
| 3. ran | 7. threw | 11. wore | 15. grew | 19. sent |
| 4. spent | 8. hurt | 12. sent | 16. held | 20. threw |
| 5. grew | 9. paid | 13. held | 17. ran | |

| | | | | |
|---|---|---|---|---|
| 2. very | 5. very | 8. too | 11. too | 14. too |
| 3. too | 6. too | 9. very | 12. very | 15. very |
| 4. too | 7. very | 10. too | 13. too | |

| | | | | | |
|---|---|---|---|---|---|
| 3. t | 10. d | 17. t | 24. d | 31. d | 38. t |
| 4. t | 11. d | 18. d | 25. t | 32. t | 39. t |
| 5. d | 12. d | 19. t | 26. d | 33. d | 40. t |
| 6. d | 13. t | 20. d | 27. t | 34. t | 41. d |
| 7. d | 14. d | 21. t | 28. d | 35. t | 42. d |
| 8. t | 15. d | 22. t | 29. d | 36. t | |
| 9. t | 16. d | 23. d | 30 d | 37. d | |

| | | | | |
|---|---|---|---|---|
| 2. You're | 7. You'll | 12. don't | 17. won't | 22. weren't |
| 3. He's | 8. He'll | 13. doesn't | 18. can't | 23. There's |
| 4. She's | 9. He'll | 14. didn't | 19. isn't | 24. I'm |
| 5. They're | 10. We've | 15. didn't | 20. aren't | |
| 6. I'll | 11. She's | 16. won't | 21. wasn't | |

| | | | | |
|---|---|---|---|---|
| 2. cannot | 7. She will | 12. was not | 17. is not | 22. do not |
| 3. do not | 8. They are | 13. I am | 18. were not | 23. You are |
| 4. will not | 9. It will | 14. He is | 19. There is | 24. You will |
| 5. She is | 10. She is | 15. did not | 20. There will | |
| 6. It is | 11. will not | 16. are not | 21. does not | |

| | | | | |
|---|---|---|---|---|
| 2. sneeze | 6. sits | 10. jewel | 14. jail | 18. wheel |
| 3. sure | 7. hear | 11. feel | 15. freeze | 19. meal |
| 4. five | 8. hair | 12. pant | 16. prove | 20. leave |
| 5. save | 9. mile | 13. wears | 17. little | |

| | | | | |
|---|---|---|---|---|
| 2. for | 7. in | 12. on | 17. from | 22. for |
| 3. to | 8. at | 13. on | 18. to | 23. on |
| 4. to | 9. in | 14. at | 19. in | 24. with |
| 5. about | 10. around | 15. in | 20. for | |
| 6. for | 11. in | 16. on | 21. for | |

| | | | |
|---|---|---|---|
| 2. ran | 6. rather good | 10. pushed | 14. airplane |
| 3. head | 7. take it off | 11. waited | 15. syllable |
| 4. send | 8. best | 12. we'll | 16. w |
| 5. hurt | 9. worst | 13. steal | 17. h |

| | | | |
|---|---|---|---|
| 2. than | 8. either | 14. eat | 20. were |
| 3. anyone | 9. will you | 15. ran | 21. to understand |
| 4. is raining | 10. go | 16. could | 22. carefully |
| 5. felt | 11. are having | 17. is ringing | 23. well |
| 6. many | 12. These | 18. make | 24. an |
| 7. much | 13. from | 19. did | |

| | | | | | | | | |
|---|---|---|---|---|---|---|---|---|
| 3. third | 3rd | 7. seventh | 7th | 11. eleventh | 11th | 15. twentieth | 20th |
| 4. fourth | 4th | 8. eighth | 8th | 12. twelfth | 12th | 16. twenty-first | 21st |
| 5. fifth | 5th | 9. ninth | 9th | 13. thirteenth | 13th | 17. twenty-fifth | 25th |
| 6. sixth | 6th | 10. tenth | 10th | 14. eighteenth | 18th | 18. thirtieth | 30th |

| | | |
|---|---|---|
| 2. does not speak | 8. are not having | 14. does not play |
| 3. did not speak | 9. is not raining | 15. must not tell |
| 4. cannot speak | 10. is not ringing | 16. may not wait |
| 5. is not | 11. does not blow | 17. did not write |
| 6. did not go | 12. will not be | 18. is not |
| 7. was not | 13. did not bring | |

2. Did he leave
3. Is she
4. Did they visit
5. Will he be
6. Is someone knocking
7. Were they

8. Was Rudy
9. Are we going to study
10. Is it going to rain?
11. Is there
12. Did he speak
13. Does she speak

14. Is Patricia
15. Do they study
16. Can she meet
17. Must we write

## Exercise 106

| | | | | | | | | | | | | |
|---|---|---|---|---|---|---|---|---|---|---|---|---|
| 2. | 3 | 1st | 8. | 3 | 2nd | 14. | 3 | 1st | 20. | 3 | 1st |
| 3. | 2 | 2nd | 9. | 5 | 3rd | 15. | 4 | 3rd | 21. | 2 | 1st |
| 4. | 3 | 2nd | 10. | 4 | 3rd | 16. | 4 | 2nd | 22. | 5 | 3rd |
| 5. | 5 | 3rd | 11. | 3 | 1st | 17. | 2 | 2nd | 23. | 2 | 1st |
| 6. | 4 | 3rd | 12. | 3 | 1st | 18. | 2 | 1st | 24. | 3 | 1st |
| 7. | 3 | 2nd | 13. | 3 | 2nd | 19. | 3 | 1st | | | |

## Exercise 107

| | | | | | |
|---|---|---|---|---|---|
| 3. irreg | 10. reg | 17. reg | 24. reg | 31. reg | 38. irreg |
| 4. reg | 11. reg | 18. irreg | 25. irreg | 32. irreg | 39. reg |
| 5. reg | 12. irreg | 19. irreg | 26. irreg | 33. irreg | 40. reg |
| 6. irreg | 13. irreg | 20. irreg | 27. reg | 34. irreg | 41. reg |
| 7. irreg | 14. irreg | 21. reg | 28. reg | 35. reg | 42. irreg |
| 8. irreg | 15. reg | 22. irreg | 29. irreg | 36. irreg | 43. reg |
| 9. reg | 16. reg | 23. irreg | 30. reg | 37. reg | 44. irreg |

## Exercise 108

2. one pound (*libra*)
3. one mile
4. seven ante meridiem
5. six post meridiem
6. five tenths
7. one half
8. one fourth/quarter
9. six percent
10. number five
11. sixty-eight degrees
12. alternating current
13. direct current
14. et cetera
15. one gallon
16. television
17. cash on delivery

18. quart
19. pint
20. yard
21. inch
22. and
23. Incorporated
24. two years
25. four feet
26. Seventh Street
27. Avenue
28. Boulevard
29. Road
30. Building
31. February
32. August
33. December

34. square feet
35. first
36. third
37. seventh
38. Thursday
39. Wednesday
40. frequency modulation
41. National Broadcasting Company
42. New York
43. Pennsylvania
44. District of Columbia
45. Maryland
46. Michigan
47. California
48. Illinois

| | | | |
|---|---|---|---|
| | 12. in | 17. in | 22. in |
| .or | 13. from | 18. in | 23. into |
| ,. for | 14. in | 19. on | 24. into |
| 10. for | 15. in | 20. for | |
| 11. over | 16. for | 21. by | |

110

| | | |
|---|---|---|
| .ovember | 10. those | 17. Portuguese |
| . five | 11. three | 18. one syllable |
| 4. third | 12. four | 19. winter |
| 5. won't | 13. ten | 20. Sunday |
| 6. cut | 14. twelve | 21. Thursday |
| 7. hit | 15. Chicago | 22. fifty-two |
| 8. Alaska | 16. Mississippi River | 23. July 4th |
| 9. north | | |

Exercise 111

| | | | |
|---|---|---|---|
| 2. hit | 6. grammar | 10. l | 14. weight |
| 3. toy | 7. broom | 11. l | 15. penny |
| 4. visit | 8. near | 12. visit | 16. choose |
| 5. very tired | 9. behind | 13. tea | 17. finally |

Exercise 112

| | | | |
|---|---|---|---|
| 2. comes | 8. than | 13. Not | 18. makes |
| 3. were | 9. warmer | 14. her | 19. he is |
| 4. have | 10. perfectly | 15. us | 20. easily |
| 5. many | 11. me to go | 16. an | 21. brings |
| 6. from | 12. anyone | 17. is beginning | 22. These |
| 7. a | | | |

Exercise 113

| | | | |
|---|---|---|---|
| 2. mine | 8. yours | 13. ours | 18. mine |
| 3. hers | 9. mine | 14. hers | 19. yours |
| 4. ours | 10. hers | 15. ours | 20. mine |
| 5. mine | 11. his | 16. yours | 21. yours |
| 6. yours | 12. mine | 17. theirs | 22. his |
| 7. theirs | | | |

Exercise 114

| | | | |
|---|---|---|---|
| 2. herself | 6. herself | 10. himself | 14. himself/herself |
| 3. myself | 7. yourself | 11. herself | 15. itself |
| 4. himself | 8. itself | 12. myself | 16. ourselves |
| 5. ourselves | 9. himself/herself | 13. yourself | 17. herself |

2. by myself
3. by himself
4. by yourself
5. by themselves
6. by ourselves
7. by herself
8. by itself
9. by himself
10. by himself
11. by yourself
12. by herself
13. by herself
14. by themselves
15. by themselves
16. by myself
17. by themselves
18. by themselves
19. by herself
20. by ourselves

2. have finished
3. have been
4. have heard
5. have been
6. have learned
7. have lost
8. has studied
9. have cleaned
10. have given
11. has been
12. have driven
13. has made
14. have captured
15. has taught
16. have seen
17. has lent
18. have read

2. lived
3. studied
4. has been
5. began
6. have studied
7. studied
8. has spoken
9. has been
10. were
11. have lived
12. lived
13. started
14. has studied
15. have been
16. became

2. hasn't felt
3. hasn't worked
4. haven't read
5. hasn't studied
6. hasn't left
7. hasn't begun
8. hasn't been
9. haven't found
10. haven't spoken
11. haven't known
12. hasn't been
13. hasn't been
14. hasn't been
15. haven't been
16. haven't lived
17. hasn't been
18. haven't been
19. haven't made
20. haven't had
21. haven't known
22. hasn't mentioned

2. Have they known
3. Have they seen
4. Has he been
5. Have they lived
6. Has Helen been
7. Have they finished
8. Has the train left ?
9. Have we learned
10. Have they been
11. Has she been
12. Have they been
13. Has he lived
14. Has Janet liked
15. Have they been
16. Has the mail arrived?
17. Has the school bell rung?
18. Has he worked
19. Have they had
20. Has it been raining
21. Have all the girls left?
22. Has he had

2. said
3. said
4. tell
5. said
6. said
7. told
8. said
9. tells
10. said

| | | | | | |
|---|---|---|---|---|---|
| | | 19. began | begun | 35. was/were | been |
| | | 20. broke | broken | 36. ended | ended |
| | ,ved | 21. brought | brought | 37. meant | meant |
| | nad | 22. came | come | 38. met | met |
| | made | 23. cost | cost | 39. read | read |
| | found | 24. did | done | 40. rode | ridden |
| | grown | 25. ate | eaten | 41. rang | rung |
| .eft | left | 26. fell | fallen | 42. ran | run |
| ₁. walked | walked | 27. felt | felt | 43. sold | sold |
| 12. showed | shown | 28. studied | studied | 44. talked | talked |
| 13. said | said | 29. lived | lived | 45. shook | shaken |
| 14. learned | learned | 30. flew | flown | 46. slept | slept |
| 15. used | used | 31. forgot | forgotten | 47. spoke | spoken |
| 16. told | told | 32. gave | given | 48. took | taken |
| 17. brought | brought | 33. went | gone | | |
| 18. waited | waited | 34. heard | heard | | |

## Exercise 122

2. did not go
3. have not delivered
4. is not beginning
5. is not
6. did not leave
7. will not return
8. does not have
9. has not gone

10. was not
11. did not prepare
12. does not come
13. is not
14. has not studied
15. did not begin
16. did not wait
17. did not tell

18. will not be
19. am not going
20. has not worked
21. cannot speak
22. must not tell
23. does not write
24. did not put

## Exercise 123

2. Do they live
3. Did he go
4. Will he be
5. Does Helen want
6. Is she
7. Is she going to study
8. Did Mr. Sanchez lend
9. Did you see

10. Was his wife
11. Was the bus
12. Do they have
13. Did she write
14. Has she studied
15. Does he have
16. Is the wind blowing
17. Can she speak

18. Do they go
19. Have they seen
20. Must he come back
21. Did she throw
22. Was he
23. Do they sit
24. Is she feeling

## Exercise 124

2. gave her brother
3. sent us
4. brought her
5. wrote Penny
6. gave us
7. told us

8. sent Betty
9. brought her
10. gave each of us
11. took her
12. lent me
13. sold his friend

14. bought his son
15. bring me
16. gave Patricia
17. paid me
18. told Leo

| | | | | |
|---|---|---|---|---|
| 2. bottom | 12. bring | 22. man | 32. daughter | 42. rough |
| 3. old | 13. inside | 23. laugh | 33. late | 43. last |
| 4. beautiful | 14. soft | 24. sour | 34. rich | 44. back |
| 5. often | 15. sharp | 25. poor | 35. near | 45. different |
| 6. sell | 16. pull | 26. white | 36. careful | 46. south |
| 7. asleep | 17. narrow | 27. many | 37. difficult | 47. east |
| 8. lend | 18. full | 28. happy | 38. worse | 48. cool |
| 9. loose | 19. thin | 29. present | 39. worst | 49. cold |
| 10. low | 20. in front of | 30. weak | 40. wet | 50. up |
| 11. cry | 21. cheap | 31. start/begin | 41. downstairs | |

| | | | | |
|---|---|---|---|---|
| 1. noun | 3. noun | 5. noun | 7. noun | 9. verb |
| 2. noun | verb | verb | verb | noun |
| verb | 4. verb | 6. verb | 8. verb | |
| noun | noun | noun | | |

| | | | |
|---|---|---|---|
| 2. collection | 12. excitement | 23. satisfy | 33. protect |
| 3. arrival | 13. death | 24. laugh | 34. discover |
| 4. decision | 14. choice | 25. grow | 35. explode |
| 5. proof | 15. growth | 26. exist | 36. imagine |
| 6. agreement | 16. marriage | 27. prove | 37. lose |
| 7. belief | 17. entrance | 28. agree | 38. fail |
| 8. punishment | 18. beginning | 29. arrive | 39. enter |
| 9. remainder | 19. appearance | 30. locate | 40. begin |
| ~~loss~~ loss | 20. repetition | 31. appear | |
| 11. ervation | 22. explain | 32. arrange | |

| | | |
|---|---|---|
| 2. turn off | 8. leave it | 14. try to find it |
| 3. enter it | 9. remove it | 15. satisfactory |
| 4. prefer to study | 10. sit down | 16. gradually |
| 5. immediately | 11. finally | 17. get information about |
| 6. telephone | 12. extremely tired | 18. be careful |
| 7. visit | 13. exactly here | |